D1424047

Travel, Gender, and Imperialism

MARY KINGSLEY AND WEST AFRICA

Alison Blunt

THE GUILFORD PRESS
New York   London

© 1994 Alison Blunt

Published by The Guilford Press
A Division of Guilford Publications, Inc.
72 Spring Street, New York, NY 10012

All rights reserved

No part of this book may be reproduced, stored in a retrieval
system, or transmitted, in any form or by any means, electronic,
mechanical, photocopying, microfilming, recording, or
otherwise, without written permission from the Publisher.

Marketed and distributed outside North America by Longman
Group UK Limited

Printed in the United States of America

This book is printed on acid-free paper.

Last digit is print number: 9 8 7 6 5 4 3 2 1

Library of Congress Cataloging-in-Publication Data

Blunt, Alison.
    Travel, gender, and imperialism : Mary Kingsley and West Africa /
Alison Blunt.
        p. cm.
    Includes bibliographical references and index.
    ISBN 0-89862-347-2. — ISBN 0-89862-546-7 (pbk.)
    1. Kingsley, Mary Henriette, 1862–1900–Journeys–Africa, West.
2. Women travelers–Africa–Biography. 3. Africa, West–Description
and travel–1850–1950. I. Title.
DT476.23.K56B58 1994
916.604'312–dc20   94-2306
                                                                  CIP

For my parents

ACKNOWLEDGMENTS

My research has been funded by the university graduate fellowship at the University of British Columbia I held from 1990 to 1993. I am indebted to Derek Gregory for his support, insight, and enthusiasm at Cambridge and at UBC, particularly while I have been writing this book. I am also very grateful to Gerry Pratt for her thought-provoking criticisms. Robyn Dowling has been a constant friend and has made many helpful comments on much of my work. I am also grateful to Sarah Jain, Natalie Jamieson, Joan Muskett, Richard Phillips, Suzy Reimer, Juliet Rowson, and Anna Skeels. My family—Cecily, Peter, and David Blunt, Stella Edridge, and Margaret Darlaston—have been particularly supportive and encouraging.

For their help in my research, I am grateful to Gwynydd Gosling at the Highgate Literary and Scientific Institute and Christine Kelly at the Royal Geographical Society. I am also grateful to Paul Jance for drawing the maps and to Mrs. B. E. Johnson at the Royal Commonwealth Society Library and Chris Wright at the Royal Anthropological Institute for their help in tracing photographs.

I am very privileged to have had access to the research of the late Beth Urquhart. She traced and transcribed hundreds of letters written by Mary Kingsley (the originals of which are located all over Britain and Ireland) and collected diverse secondary sources. I fully appreciate her years of conscientious research, which have proved invaluable for my work. I am grateful to her daughter, Sarah Urquhart, for giving me permission to study Beth Urquhart's collection, and to Alvin Urquhart for his kind hospitality in letting me work in his home.

I was very lucky to learn about this material, and the chain of coincidences resulting in two visits to Eugene, Oregon, is worth repeating. I had known of Beth Urquhart through her friendship with Gwynydd Gosling, but was unaware of the scale of her research. Mona Domosh presented a paper on women travel writers at the Association of American Geographers Conference in Miami in 1991, which was attended by Alvin Urquhart, a Professor of Geography at the University of Oregon in Eugene. He told her of his late wife's research on Mary Kingsley and that he had several boxes of transcribed letters in his basement. Mona Domosh had heard about my interests through Gerry Pratt, and wrote to tell her of this source. I traveled to Eugene and was overwhelmed by the scale of Beth Urquhart's research. The Bibliography lists her transcriptions of hundreds of letters and fragments of letters written by Mary Kingsley.

CONTENTS

"Only a Woman . . ."

.

In this book I consider the travels and travel writing of Mary Kingsley, who, on her return to Britain from two journeys in West Africa, became a well-known figure in imperial debates of the 1890s.[1]

This chapter's title, "Only a Woman," comes from a letter Kingsley wrote to Joseph Chamberlain, the British colonial secretary, in April 1898. The phrase raises three themes central to the study of imperial travel writing by women. First, its derogatory tone suggests the prevalent patriarchal constructions of women as weak and inferior, as echoed by Kingsley in writing

> I am only a woman and we ladies—though great on details and concrete conceptions—are never capable of feeling a devotion to things I know well enough are really greater namely abstract things.[2]

Second, "Only a Woman" has potential for a more positive tone of admiration for the achievements of women travelers so long neglected. Finally, "Only a Woman" highlights the social, ideological, and logistical significance of women traveling alone.

I want to show that these three themes are inseparable. I draw on poststructuralist and feminist theories, illustrating their importance for writing historical geographies and histories of geography. Before introducing more specific questions, I begin by outlining distinct yet interrelated contexts for my study. These include both women as a focus of historical research and the study of Western women and imperialism, and also the imperialist underpinnings of nineteenth-century British geography and the place of women within a historiography of geography.

1

WOMEN'S HISTORIES

Joan Scott has traced a genealogy of historical studies of women, highlighting three approaches.[3] The earliest stages of "women's history" were marked by essentialist, often positivist accounts that simply added "women's experience" to historical inquiry.[4] Initially,

> women's history . . . sought to challenge traditional, masculinist, "objective" "history" by making women visible, by writing women into "history." That "history," however, was in most other respects informed by traditional, thus masculinist, categories and historical periods and reflected masculinist values.[5]

"Values" such as reason and rationality had been constructed as masculine since the Enlightenment, when perceptions of a split between mind and body posited knowledge as autonomous and objective.[6] Second, social history stimulated new methods and new areas of research relevant for writing women's histories. Although women had been largely excluded from narratives of political history and were now a focus of research, human agency more generally was arguably reduced to a function of economic forces. Finally, Scott describes attempts to conceptualize gender and suggests the need to redefine basic terms of analysis such as subject, gender, and politics.

As one way of redefining such terms of analysis, poststructuralism suggests that women and gender relations should not only become visible in historical study but should "remake the very categories through which the past is discursively constituted."[7] In its broadest terms, poststructuralism can offer

> a new way of analyzing constructions of meaning and relationships of power that called unitary, universal categories into question and historicized concepts otherwise treated as natural (such as man/woman) or absolute (such as equality or justice).[8]

Rather than offer an introduction to poststructuralism, I am working with it, as should become apparent throughout the book.[9] I emphasize time- and place-specific constructions of difference along lines of, most notably, gender, race, and class. In my consideration of decentered subjectivity, I most specifically address poststructuralist claims for the "death of the author" in Chapter 2.

Throughout, I attempt to deconstruct binary oppositions such as home/away and colonizer/colonized, instead revealing their ambivalence and contestation. The inseparability of power and "knowledge" informs my arguments about British imperialism and discursive constructions of femininity and masculinity in the late nineteenth century.

At this stage, however, I want simply to highlight two poststructuralist concerns that seem particularly important for writing women's histories. These are, first, that history represents a range of discontinuous and disconnected discourses and, second, the fluid constitution of subjectivity within such discourses. Following Michel Foucault, I assume that discourse represents "a historically, socially, and institutionally specific structure of statements, terms, categories, and beliefs."[10] Discursive rules and formations change over time, as shown by, for example, the changing discourses of madness and sexuality.[11] Such discourses inform subjectivity because

> the fragmented, unstable subject of poststructuralism is not regarded as a rational autonomous unit producing meanings and values, but rather as being constituted in the ebb and flow of conflicting meanings generated by various discourses.[12]

Unlike accounts that merely add a gendered subject, the construction of subjectivity itself becomes a central point of inquiry. For many feminists, this poses a dilemma between recognizing both gender and subjectivity as constructed and the strategic need to assert gendered subjectivity.[13]

For Denise Riley, the category "women" is constructed and hence unstable, constantly produced and reworked over time.[14] In addressing the feminist need to concentrate on and yet refuse the identity "women," she emphasizes both the discursive formations of history and the historicity of discursive formations:

> It's not that our identity is to be dissipated into airy indeterminacy, extinction; instead it is to be referred to the more substantial realms of discursive historical formation.[15]

In my view, poststructuralism offers the potential for feminist history to become, in the words of Scott, "not just an attempt to correct or supplement an incomplete record of the past but a way of critically understanding how history operates as a site of the production of gender knowledge."[16] But this is more than a matter of restructuring and recomposing history. Scott's reference to a "site" is part of a more general and intrinsically spatial imagery that both she and Riley widely employ.[17] For example, Scott refers to epistemological and institutional space for feminist research in the humanities generally and, more specifically, in poststructuralist critiques of empiricism and humanism. Within her own work, she states that gender has been neglected in political history to such an extent that "the territory is virtually uncharted."[18] This spatial imagery is echoed by Riley, who writes, for example, that "women" "are embedded in a new topography, which does not have a conscious past. So they are figures in a landscape, rather than episodes in a history."[19] I hope to transcend what seems to me a discrete and somewhat rigid compartmentalization by revealing the fluid and inseparable relations of—and between—spatiality and temporality. For both Scott and Riley, spatial imagery is cited in a largely rhetorical way, revealing more about imagery generally than spatiality specifically. In contrast, I address the spatiality integral to such images, and I consider how discursive formations are constructed and unstable over space as well as over time.

Relating both to spatial imagery and to discursive discontinuities over space, a notion of subject positionality can overcome "the dilemma between a post-structuralist genderless subject and a cultural feminist essentialized subject."[20] Subject positionality makes it "both possible and desirable to construe a gendered subjectivity in relation to concrete habits, practices, and discourses while at the same time recognizing the fluidity of these."[21] I consider subject positionality in terms of constructions of race and class as well as gender, revealing their complexities over space and time. Overall, I want to consider how both space and subjectivity are complex and fluid rather than transparent and fixed in constructing subject positionality.[22]

My focus on Mary Kingsley thus relates to subject positionality rather than any realist claims to biographical authenticity and/or authority. Rather than celebrate an individual, I hope that through my textual and contextual interrogations I can address constructions of subjectivity more broadly. Attempts to reclaim feminist "heroines" from the past perpetuate rather than challenge traditional masculinist and humanist categories of analysis by isolating individual subjects from their discursive contexts.[23] However, biographical studies can provide positions or sites for representing the complexities of such discursive contexts. For Scott, the most successful research so far in examining "the ways in which gendered identities are substantively constructed"[24] has been biographical. As Biddy Martin found in her study of Lou Andreas-Salomé,

> the suppression of biographical and social contingency in favor of an exclusive study of texts has not undone the traditional biographical monumentalization of modern male literary giants. Nor has it ended the marginalization of women writers and intellectuals. . . . In Salomé I find a concrete historical site and a set of texts that allow for the exploration of sexual difference, intellectual debt, and self-representation from within the specific biographical and intellectual constellations in which Salomé's work was located.[25]

In my focus on Kingsley, I hope to emphasize subject positionality in terms of constructions of, primarily, gender, race, and class and how she was represented over space and time by her own and others' writings at "home" and abroad in the context of British imperialism.

WESTERN WOMEN AND IMPERIALISM

Recent studies of Western women and imperialism reflect many of the themes underlying attempts to move beyond "women's history." Different overviews have revealed the many diverse roles that women have played in imperial contexts but that have traditionally been ignored or downplayed.[26] Recent interest in white women in colonial settings has often taken the form of romantic, nostalgic imagery in literature, television, and film, notably since the 1980s.[27] This interest has been supported by historiographical foundations that represent

> the latest reconstruction of imperial history, one which rejects the notion of the empire as male space or of imperial history as what the policy makers in London planned. Thus, the fields of women's history and imperial history have intersected.[28]

These approaches isolate and often celebrate individual "heroic" women rather than question constructions of gender in both the metaphorically colonial context of patriarchal inequality and the more literal places and spaces of colonization. Similarly, by neglecting differences in the construction of gendered subjectivities, such approaches totalize the experiences of colonized women and silence what postcolonial perspectives seek to assert.[29]

In her work on white women, racism, and history, Vron Ware has studied histories of slavery and imperialism

> not to bring white women to account for past misdeeds, nor to search for heroines whose reputations can help to absolve the rest from guilt, but to find out how white women negotiated questions of race and racism—as well as class and gender.[30]

According to Jane Haggis, however, the study of colonial women is inherently contradictory. On one level, to isolate gender from its interactions with, for example, race and class seems essentialist. On another level, to distinguish between the behavior of white men and women toward colonized people is also essentialist but is dependent on constructions of racial difference.[31] This contradiction means that white women become visible at the expense of colonized women, perpetuating an exclusionary, ethnocentric discourse.[32] The dichotomization between colonizing men and women should be deconstructed, and constructions of gender difference should not be isolated from, most significantly, constructions of racial difference.

GEOGRAPHICAL KNOWLEDGE AND IMPERIALISM

The roles played by white women in imperialism are particularly pertinent to historiographies of geography and geographical knowledge.[33] I use both terms because I do not want to confine the meaning of geography to a formal academic discipline. In the same spirit, Mona Domosh has attempted to use women travelers to outline a feminist historiography of geography. She states, however, that "geography's roots in the exploratory tradition are . . . quite inspiring and should act as sources of pride,"[34] and she tries to add women travelers to this tradition without addressing the imperialist implications of such a project.

In his focus on the institutionalization of geography in late nineteenth-century Europe, Felix Driver points to the neglect of the connections between geography and imperialism, particularly compared with other disciplines such as anthropology.[35] In largely instrumental terms, it can of course be argued that "geography was the science of imperialism *par excellence*" because "exploration, topographic and social survey, cartographic representation, and regional inventory . . . were entirely suited to the colonial project."[36] But because imperialism was about far more than economic exploitation, Driver calls for critical, contextual histories of geography relating to "the *culture* of imperialism."[37] He goes on to write that "contemporary writings on 'geography' were infused with assumptions about gender, as well as empire; to ignore the former is necessarily to misinterpret the latter,"[38] as illustrated by imperial representations of masculinity. It is equally the case, however, that to ignore assumptions about empire when studying the institutionalization of late nineteenth-century British geography is to misinterpret assumptions about gender. This returns to my earlier criticism of Domosh's attempt to map women onto a historiography of geography while addressing neither the imperial foundations of geography nor the imperial context that facilitated the travels of the British women she cites.

In reply to Domosh, David Stoddart suggests that "the contribution of women to the emergence and development of geography as a formal academic discipline"[39] would be more relevant to a feminist historiography of geography. But in the late nineteenth century, institutions outside the academy were important in shaping perceptions of both women travelers and their travels and hence in establishing a wider constituency for geographical knowledge. In the Postlude I focus on the debates about admitting women as fellows to Britain's Royal Geographical Society (RGS) in the 1890s. At this stage, however, I want to introduce the pivotal role of the RGS in forging connections between "new imperialism" and "new geography."

The RGS was founded in 1830 with a membership of travelers, explorers, and titled (often military) men.[40] From about 1870, Stoddart has argued, an emergent "new geography" was characterized by increased professionalization and the movement to establish geography as a formal academic discipline. By the 1880s and 1890s, though, the increased specialization of other disciplines, notably geology, meant that although British geography was emerging as a scientific discipline, institutions such as the RGS lacked, in Stoddart's words, "strictly scientific men."[41] Calls for geographical education often reflected imperialist imperatives. For example, in 1885 John Scott Keltie, who had been commissioned by the RGS to report on the state of geographical education in Britain, wrote:

> There is no country that can less afford to dispense with geographical knowledge than England . . . [yet] there are few countries in which a high order of geographical teaching is so little encouraged. The interests of England are wide as the world. Her colonies, her commerce, her emigrations, her wars, her missionaries, and her scientific explorers bring her into contact with all parts of the globe, and it is therefore a matter of imperial importance that no reasonable means should be neglected of training her youth in sound geographical knowledge.[42]

These imperial objectives were not the unique preserve of the RGS in London; its members were by no means confined to the metropolis, and there was at the same time a remarkably vigorous growth of geographical societies in the provinces. John MacKenzie has shown that as imperialism moved from exploration to commerce, so provincial geographical societies were founded

> as pressure groups for imperialism, concerned with a more practical and ideologically committed geography than their metropolitan predecessor, and with an educational and scholarly programme designed to further the interests of the imperial state.[43]

Membership of these societies grew rapidly at first but declined from the 1890s, and only the Scottish and Manchester geographical societies survived beyond World War II. Unlike in the RGS, women had always been admitted to these societies.

In contrast to both Domosh and Stoddart, I believe that it is essential to study the roles played by women in the historiography of geography, but that this should question the very basis of that historiography rather than reproduce it in a revised form. Gender should not be seen in essentialist terms but rather as constructed and contested in many different ways over space and time. Ultimately, this should reflect on the imperialist foundations of geography as an academic discipline, raising questions concerning the practice of writing histories, geographies, and historiographies.

*   *   *

I hope that these contexts—women as a focus of historical research, studying Western women and imperialism, and the place of women in a historiography of geography—are both implicitly and explicitly significant throughout my account. More specifically, I address four inseparable concerns: the distinctive characteristics of travel writing by women; how these reflected and reproduced spatial differentiation, notably between spheres of patriarchal and imperial power and authority; how the subject positions of women travel writers were constructed in terms of difference, primarily along lines of gender, race, and class, and how such constructions varied over space and time; and how women's journeys represented only one moment in their travels and subsequent writings. I focus on the travels and writings of Mary Kingsley, but rather than celebrate her as an individual, I stress gendered subjectivity and its relations to broader discursive formations.

In Chapter 1 I discuss the metaphorical and material significance of travel and travel writing; the distinctive nature of imperial literary representation; and how both travel writing and, more broadly, imperial representations were differentiated by constructions of gender. I hope to demonstrate the immanence of ambivalence in the construction of subjectivity to avoid reproducing imperial totalizations of "otherness." I introduce the life, travels, and writings of Kingsley in the Interlude before focusing on her departure, journey, and return in the remaining chapters.

In Chapter 2 I assess departure in the sense of constructions of gendered subjectivity both prior to and during Kingsley's journeys. Women's travels often differed from those of men, as shown by the preparation of "conduct books," the motives for travel and travel writing, and the scale and goals of the journey. In terms of textual representations of difference, I focus on Kingsley's accounts of herself and others, notably African women, as gendered subjects. By considering "Space, Place, and Imperial Subjectivity" in Chapter 3, I seek to illustrate the ambivalence of and interplay between constructions of racial and gender difference. I address the ambiguities of women travelers' being constructed as subordinate in terms of gender in the context of patriarchal society but able in their travels to share in the authority of colonizers defined primarily in terms of racial difference. In particular, I discuss Kingsley's perceptions of colonized places (her landscape descriptions) and people (her perceptions of racial difference).

The final moment shaping and indeed defining Kingsley's travels was her reconstitution of "home" on her return, which I discuss in Chapter 4. I illustrate the ways in which her political position prompted the coexistence of public and private spheres of influence, and how her marginality as a woman again gained preeminence in perceptions of her travels, writings, and politics. I draw upon many published book reviews and obituaries to reflect upon her reception on her return. As a postlude to this, I discuss two examples of more institutional responses to women travel writers. The debates surrounding the admission of women as fellows of the RGS and the political and literary construction of "new women" may seem tangential to Kingsley's life and travels but are important in revealing the conditions and constraints for women able to travel in the 1890s.

Imperial women's travel writing was distinctive in the ways that women traveled, how they wrote about their travels, and how their writings were received. In my focus on Mary Kingsley, I do not want to perpetuate celebratory stereotypes of an intrepid individual. Rather, this specific focus relates to broader themes and contexts, underpinned by the immanence of poststructuralism and feminism to both historical geography and histories of geography. I reveal the interplay of the three potential interpretations of the phrase "only a woman" so that rather than merely add a gendered subject to geography and historiography, I can, more importantly, consider subjectivity itself.

NOTES

1. See the Interlude for a fuller introduction to Kingsley herself.
2. Kingsley to Chamberlain, April 30, 1898. See the first section of the bibliography to this volume for a list of archival sources.
3. J. W. Scott, *Gender and the Politics of History* (New York: Columbia University Press, 1988b).

4. M. Valverde, "Poststructuralist Gender Historians: Are We Those Names?" *Labour/Le Travail* 25 (Spring 1990): 227–236.

5. J. Newton, "History as Usual? Feminism and the 'New Historicism,'" *Cultural Critique* 9 (Spring 1988): 87–121; p. 100.

6. See G. Rose, *Feminism and Geography: The Limits of Geographical Knowledge* (Cambridge, England: Polity Press, 1993) for a critique of the masculinism in geography that draws on the same "values" as a masculinist history.

7. J. Howard, "Feminism and the Question of History: Resituating the Debate," *Women's Studies* 19 (1991): 149–157; p. 151. See also M. C. Howell, "A New Feminist Historian Looks at the New Historicism: What's So Historical about It?" *Women's Studies* 19 (1991): 139–147. She writes that "women's history, by definition, is an effort to restore to the historical record material which traditional histories have ignored, effaced, or misrepresented. With such material, we hope to unearth the ideological and social worlds that have constructed separate genders, to explore the distinct interests and agencies at work in these constructions, and finally to transform our understanding of the past" (p. 140).

8. J. W. Scott, "Deconstructing Equality-Versus-Difference: or, The Uses of Poststructuralist Theory for Feminism," *Feminist Studies* 14 (1988a): 33–50; p. 33. This includes clear summaries of language, discourse, difference, and deconstruction, which she describes as "among the useful terms feminists have appropriated from post-structuralism" (p. 34).

9. Poststructuralism clearly denotes a complex and contested terrain that is beyond the scope of this Introduction. For overviews that are particularly relevant for this context, see *Post-structuralism and the Question of History*, ed. D. Attridge, G. Bennington, and R. Young (Cambridge, England: Cambridge University Press, 1987); *Textual Strategies: Perspectives in Poststructuralist Criticism*, ed. J. V. Harari (Ithaca, NY: Cornell University Press, 1979); C. Weedon, *Feminist Practice and Poststructuralist Theory* (Oxford, England: Basil Blackwell, 1987); and *Untying the Text: A Post-structuralist Reader*, ed. R. Young (Boston: Routledge and Kegan Paul, 1981). Weedon writes (pp. 12–13): "The theories which have helped produce poststructuralism include the structural linguistics of Ferdinand de Saussure and Emile Benveniste, Marxism, particularly Louis Althusser's theory of ideology, and the psychoanalysis of Sigmund Freud and Jacques Lacan. They also include Jacques Derrida's theory of *différance*, with its critique of the metaphysics of presence, in which the speaking subject's intention guarantees meaning, and language is a tool for expressing something beyond it, the deconstruction based on Derrida's theory and Michel Foucault's theory of discourse and power."

10. Scott 1988a, 35.

11. See, for example, M. Foucault, *The History of Sexuality*, trans. R. Hurley, vol. 1 (New York: Vintage Books, 1990). For a recent commentary on Foucault, see L. McNay, *Foucault and Feminism: Power, Gender and the Self* (Cambridge, England: Polity Press, 1992).

12. Valverde 1990, 228.

13. As discussed by L. Alcoff, "Cultural Feminism versus Post-structuralism: The Identity Crisis in Feminist Theory," *Signs* 13, 3 (1988): 405–437; and S. Hekman, "Reconstituting the Subject: Feminism, Modernism, and Postmodernism," *Hypatia* 6, 2 (1991): 44–63.

14. D. Riley, *"Am I That Name?" Feminism and the Category of "Women" in History* (London: Macmillan, 1988). Also see R. Radhakrishnan, "Feminist Historiography and Post-structuralist Thought," in *The Difference Within: Feminism and Critical Theory,* ed. E. Meese and A. Parker (Amsterdam: John Benjamins, 1989). He writes that "without the benefit of post-structuralist theory, feminist historiography . . . is in danger of turning into a superficial reversal of forces of power that would leave untouched certain general and underlying economies of meaning and history" (p. 189) but stresses a political imperative to go beyond poststructuralism.

15. Riley 1988, 5.

16. Scott 1988b, 10.

17. For further discussion of feminist uses of spatial imagery—specifically mapping—in colonial and postcolonial contexts, see A. Blunt and G. Rose, "Introduction: Women's Colonial and Post-colonial Geographies," in *Sexual/Textual Colonizations: Women's Colonial and Post-colonial Geographies,* ed. A. Blunt and G. Rose (New York: Guilford Press, forthcoming).

18. Scott 1988b, 46.

19. Riley 1988, 49.

20. Alcoff 1988, 423. Alcoff discusses the work of Denise Riley and Teresa de Lauretis in this context.

21. Ibid., 431.

22. See Blunt and Rose, forthcoming, Chapter 1, for a critique of transparency.

23. This is well illustrated by an account of feminist historical biography writing, when "unpalatable facts" are often unavoidable. See, for example, D. Birkett and J. Wheelwright, "'How Could She?' Unpalatable Facts and Feminists' Heroines," *Gender and History* 2, 1 (1990): 49–57. They write, "Rather than explaining [unpalatable facts] away, we began to incorporate them into our subjects' biographies, making them integral rather than peripheral to our understanding of them. Our portraits became not those of simple feminist heroines, but of women rooted in their time, illuminating not only women's lives but the period in which they lived" (p. 50). They also write that "to rewrite history to conform more exactly with current received notions of feminist thought serves to obscure rather than to clarify the past. . . . Only by allowing these historical figures to live within their context, expressing views with which we might violently disagree, can we understand them."

24. Scott 1988b, 44.

25. B. Martin, *Woman and Modernity: The (Life)Styles of Lou Andreas-Salomé* (Ithaca, NY: Cornell University Press, 1991), 2.

26. See, for example, the special edition of *Women's Studies International Forum* 13, 4 (1990). Many of these essays were reprinted, together with others, in *Western Women and Imperialism: Complicity and Resistance*, ed. N. Chaudhuri and M. Strobel (Bloomington: Indiana University Press, 1992). For a concise yet broad overview, see M. Strobel, *European Women and the Second British Empire* (Bloomington: Indiana University Press, 1991).

27. N. Chaudhuri and M. Strobel, "Western Women and Imperialism: Introduction," *Women's Studies International Forum* 13, 4 (1990): 289–293; p. 289.

28. Chaudhuri and Strobel 1990, 290.

29. G. C. Spivak, "Three Women's Texts and a Critique of Imperialism," *Critical Inquiry* 12 (Autumn 1985): 243–261. Also see Blunt and Rose, forthcoming; G. C. Spivak, *The Post-colonial Critic: Interviews, Strategies, Dialogues*, ed. S. Harasym (London: Routledge, 1990); and T. T. Minh-ha, *Woman, Native, Other: Writing Postcoloniality and Feminism* (Bloomington: Indiana University Press, 1989).

30. V. Ware, *Beyond the Pale: White Women, Racism and History* (London: Verso, 1992), 43.

31. J. Haggis, "Gendering Colonialism or Colonising Gender? Recent Women's Studies Approaches to White Women and the History of British Colonialism," *Women's Studies International Forum* 13, 1/2 (1990): 105–115.

32. Ibid.

33. See G. Rose and M. Ogborn, "Feminism and Historical Geography," *Journal of Historical Geography* 14, 4 (1988): 405–409 for an introduction to feminist historical geography.

34. M. Domosh, "Toward a Feminist Historiography of Geography," *Transactions of the Institute of British Geographers* N.S. 16 (1991a): 95–104; p. 95. See Chapter 2 for further discussion of imperial exploration and how it has been constructed as distinct from travel.

35. F. Driver, "Geography's Empire: Histories of Geographical Knowledge," *Environment and Planning D: Society and Space* 10 (1992): 23–40.

36. D. Livingstone, *The Geographical Tradition: Episodes in the History of a Contested Enterprise* (Oxford, England: Basil Blackwell, 1993), 160 and 170. The "tradition" that Livingstone outlines is, unfortunately, all too traditional in its masculinism. See Rose 1993 for the most recent attempt to contest such an "enterprise."

37. Driver 1992, my emphasis. See Chapter 1 for discussion of Edward Said's work on "the culture of imperialism" and the significance of travel writing as a channel for imperial representations.

38. Driver 1992, 28.

39. D. R. Stoddart, "Do We Need a Feminist Historiography of Geography—and if We Do, What Should It Be?" *Transactions of the Institute of British Geographers* N.S. 16 (1991): 484–487; p. 485. Also see

Domosh's reply to this: M. Domosh, "Beyond the Frontiers of Geographical Knowledge," *Transactions of the Institute of British Geographers* N.S. 16 (1991b): 488–490; p. 489.

40. D. R. Stoddart, *On Geography and Its History* (Oxford, England: Basil Blackwell, 1986).

41. Stoddart 1986, 67.

42. J. S. Keltie, "Report to the Council of the Royal Geographical Society on Geographical Education," *Supplementary Papers of the Royal Geographical Society* 1, 4 (1886): 439–554.

43. J. MacKenzie, "Geography and Imperialism: British Provincial Geographical Societies," in *Nature and Science: Essays in the History of Geographical Knowledge*, ed. F. Driver and G. Rose (London: Historical Geography Research Group of the Institute of British Geographers, 1992): 49–62; p. 61.

CHAPTER 1

Planning a Route

TRAVEL, TRAVEL WRITING, AND IMPERIAL REPRESENTATION

Imperial women's travel writing has to be located within the broader contexts of travel, travel writing, and imperial literary traditions. I am particularly interested in how women travel writers negotiated "home" and away in the context of British imperialism, and how constructions of gender, race, and class shaped and constrained subjectivity over space and time.

The three sections of this chapter become progressively more specific. In the first section I discuss travel and travel writing, considering the metaphorical immanence of travel as well as reading and writing travel in material terms. In the second section, I address travel writing and imperial representation and consider colonial discourses of "othering," notions of ambivalence, imperial literary traditions, and imperial representations of gender and sexuality. In the third section, I introduce imperial travel writing by women.

Two themes run throughout the chapter: the metaphorical as well as material significance of travel writing and the ambivalence of imperial representations of difference.

TRAVEL AND TRAVEL WRITING

The Metaphorical Immanence of Travel

By definition, metaphor is inherently spatial in that it connects two seemingly disconnected ideas in order to construct meaning.[1]

Explicitly spatial metaphors are particularly important in feminist and postcolonial criticism, often referring to the influences of position, notably marginality, on constructions of identity.[2] Janet Wolff has suggested that "travel" has been widely employed by cultural critics in different metaphorical ways, but she seems to be addressing metaphors of mobility generally rather than travel specifically and largely overlooks the spatiality informing both.[3] By focusing on the metaphorical significance of constructions of "home" and away, I hope, first, to show that travel can provide distinctive metaphors of mobility and, second, to stress the inherent spatiality of such metaphors.

Travel as "traveling theory" can illustrate the movement of ideas and theory away from a point of origin to a new destination, with their content changing over space and time.[4] In another way notions of travel can stimulate the self-conscious recognition of position by the researcher. James Clifford views travel as a translation term for comparative cultural studies whereby the blurring between dwelling and traveling is revealed, and "constructed and disputed *historicities*, sites of displacement, interference, and interaction, come more sharply into view."[5] Clifford proposes the use of "travel" in cultural comparison

> precisely because of its historical taintedness, its associations with gendered, racial bodies, class privilege, specific means of conveyance, beaten paths, agents, frontiers, documents, and the like. I prefer it to more apparently neutral, and "theoretical," terms, such as "displacement," which can make the drawing of equivalence across different historical experiences too easy.[6]

It is, however, ironic that such a sense of travel, and its place within broader projects of cross-cultural comparison, should reproduce constructions of difference. Travel should be seen as diverse, incorporating voluntary but also forced movement, and experienced differently along lines of race, class, and gender.[7] Cultural critique oriented around ideas of travel should be theoretically informed and substantively grounded to avoid "theoretical tourism on the part of the first world critic, where the margin becomes a linguistic or critical vacation, a new poetics of the exotic."[8]

Metaphor can figuratively overcome difference only by transporting ideas of travel to a text. This is, I think, what Georges Van den Abbeele means when he writes that travel "becomes the metaphor of metaphor while the structure of the metaphor becomes the metaphor for the travel of meaning."[9] The critical distance and perspective that can arise from the orientation and disorientation of travel relate both to seeing and knowing. Travel is bounded by points of departure and destination but in an arbitrary, retrospective way defined by perceptions of "home" that can themselves arise only with critical distance. For Van den Abbeele,

> the concept of a home is needed (and in fact it can only be thought) only *after* the home has already been left behind. In a strict sense, then, one has always already left home, since home can only exist as such at the price of it being lost.[10]

To travel is an attempt to mediate this loss by the "spatialization of time." However, to travel also represents the "temporalization of space" whereby orientation seems paradoxically disorienting because

> the point of return as repetition of the point of departure cannot take place without a difference in that repetition: the detour constitutive of the voyage itself. Were the point of departure and the point of return to remain exactly the same, that is, were they the same point, there could be no travel.[11]

Travel thus involves the familiarization or domestication of the unfamiliar at the same time as the defamiliarization of the familiar or domestic. Travel seems potentially liberating because of the opportunities for transgression and questioning of ideas formulated at home. But such transgression is bounded within the definition of travel because "the very understanding of . . . error as 'wandering' implies a topography or space of wandering."[12] The risks of travel are potentially alienating because of the dangers "of becoming a foreigner in one's own land in the case of literal travel, [and] becoming a stranger in one's own time in the case of scholarly travel."[13]

Van den Abbeele, like his traveler/theorist, seems able to move beyond home but, by recognizing it in a retrospective and arbitrary way, seems neither able nor compelled to attempt to change it. For Wolff, "just as the practices and ideologies of *actual* travel operate to exclude or pathologize women, so the use of that vocabulary as

metaphor necessarily produces androcentric tendencies in theory."[14]
Travel as metaphor seems rooted in what has historically been
a distinctly masculine tradition whereby the traveler/theorist is
able to move beyond home rather than be constrained within it.[15]
Notions of "home" should be destabilized to illustrate the unequal
access to travel and, by metaphorical extension, to theory, and
different, distinctively gendered, meanings of "home" should be
explored.[16] In addition, travel/theory relates to the Enlightenment
project of all-encompassing vision through the eyes of an individual,
supposedly rational viewer, similarly implying a masculine subject.[17]
Van den Abbeele refers to these critical issues only in passing.

In the context of poststructural and postcolonial critiques of
"knowledge," the privileging of perspectives of an elite able to
travel/theorize should be resisted by giving voice to those defined
as marginal. Indeed, it has been argued that poststructuralism "advo-
cates strongly a model of knowledge not as home or domain, but
as orphaned and exilic."[18] Metaphors of mobility have gained wide
currency in postcolonial literary criticism. For example, these can
address subjectivity in marginal spaces, as shown by Edward Said,
who writes that "liberation as an intellectual mission"

> has now shifted from the settled, established, and domesticated
> dynamics of culture, to its unhoused, decentered, and exilic energies,
> energies whose incarnation today is the migrant, and whose con-
> sciousness is that of the intellectual and artist in exile, the political
> figure between domains, between forms, *between homes*, and be-
> tween languages.[19]

Homi Bhabha has written of the "unhomely" displacement of the
modern world and discusses postcolonial attempts to position the
world in the home and the home in the world. The inscription of
in-between, hybrid spaces of "border existence" "inhabits a still-
ness of time and a strangeness of framing that creates the discursive 'image' at the crossroads of history and literature, bridging the
home and the world."[20] More specifically, Rosemary Marangoly
George has argued that an immigrant genre of literature "is marked
by a curiously detached reading of the experience of 'homelessness'
which is compensated for by an excessive use of the metaphor of
luggage, both spiritual and material."[21] Finally, linking this focus
on immigration with Said's and Bhabha's broader interest in

"home," Paul Carter has written that "an authentically migrant perspective . . . might begin by regarding movement, not as an awkward interval between fixed points of departure and arrival, but as a mode of being in the world."[22]

Feminist and postcolonial critiques suggest that metaphors of travel are inseparable from those of position and constructions of marginality that give rise to the time- and place-specific subjectivity of the traveler. This corresponds with Wolff's call for the need to situate the destabilization of androcentric—and, I would add, ethnocentric—metaphors of travel.

Reading and Writing Travel

The material nature of travel has been seen by some to lie on a historical continuum from exploration to travel to tourism, while others have attempted to deconstruct such a continuum. Although conceding "obvious overlaps," Paul Fussell has stated that "exploration belongs to the Renaissance, travel to the bourgeois age, tourism to our own proletarian moment."[23] This simplistic teleology corresponds to different motivations:

> The explorer seeks the undiscovered, the traveler that which has been discovered by the mind working in history, the tourist that which has been discovered by entrepreneurship and prepared for him [*sic*] by the arts of mass publicity. The genuine traveler is, or used to be, in the middle between the two extremes.[24]

From the perspective of contemporary Western society, travel is perhaps most commonly defined in terms of its difference from tourism. Travel seems independent, individualistic, and active, unlike the mass, essentially passive consumption associated with tourism. John Urry has mapped the infrastructure and logistics of tourism as inextricably bound up with broader socioeconomic restructuring.[25] He discusses the "tourist gaze" primarily in terms of the object that differs from everyday life rather than the characteristics enabling or constraining the viewing subject.[26]

However, to distinguish travel from tourism in these or other ways arguably creates a false distinction overlooking the material and metaphorical implications for cross-cultural representation through signification. Following Bhabha, this

is not simply a matter of language; it is the question of culture's representation of difference—manners, words, rituals, customs, time—
inscribed without a transcendent subject that knows, outside of a
mimetic social memory.[27]

For Jonathan Culler, tourists are agents of semiotics, reading cities,
landscapes, and cultures as sign systems. To distinguish between
travel and tourism, epitomized by Fussell's "hysterical smugness"
in celebrating British travel writing in the interwar period, is self-
defeating because both relate to broader notions of signification.
The construction of this distinction parallels others, including "the
authentic and the inauthentic, the natural and the touristy,"[28] which
are more tangible semiotic operators helping to structure the tourist gaze. Signification is facilitated by markers presenting sites as
sights to the viewer.[29] However, this form of representation is paradoxical because

> to be experienced as authentic it must be marked as authentic, but
> when it is marked as authentic it is mediated, a sign of itself, and hence
> lacks the authenticity of what is truly unspoiled, untouched by medi-
> ating cultural codes.[30]

Travel has been perceived as either changing over time, as
Fussell and Urry argue, or remaining essentially the same in terms
of broader processes of signification, as Culler argues. I think that
it is possible to reconcile these two positions through a poststructural and, more specifically, discursive understanding of travel.
This would reveal discontinuities over space and time whereby
exploration, travel, and tourism acquire distinct meanings while
being informed by the underlying significance of perceptions of
difference by an individual or group mediating the spheres of
"home" and away. Hence, when I refer to "travel," I am referring
to the specific context whereby women traveling alone in the late
nineteenth century were defined primarily as travelers rather than
explorers or tourists, but also the underlying context of cross-
cultural representation through signification.

Travel writing takes many diverse forms including

> the decasyllabic couplet, the discontinuous field note, the journal,
> the diary, the narrative, the report, the letter, the history, the eth-
> nography, the novel, and combinations of them.[31]

Both travel and travel writing are hermeneutic processes whereby the "eye/I" of the traveler/travel writer constructs spatial and textual difference.[32] Travel writing is distinctive because autobiographical narrative exists alongside, and seems to gain authority from, observational detail. The journey undertaken and represented can be seen as a psychological journey, relating to themes of the journey of life and self-discovery. Such self-referentiality parallels that of diary narratives because

> in much the same way as the diarist uses public or cultural codes to mitigate the split between narrating self and narrated self, he or she can also fall back on an analogy between a geographical journey and a spiritual journey: the traveller can view the journey as destined towards a place in which narrator and actor are reconciled in a visionary self-presence.[33]

However, this self-referentiality is based on constructions of difference because

> the quest for Self through a search for the Other depends on and reveals an image of the Self, an image of the Other, and, most important, a passage between them—the "wanting to know," which constitutes travel and finally becomes the narrative.[34]

Travel writing seems to mediate "fact" and fiction, often seeming to transcend conventional distinctions between scientific and literary writing. This is predicated on the authority of the author representing experiences that are not easily verifiable.[35] It can also seem that the travel writer enjoys a superior status to the reader because "the speaker in any travel book exhibits himself [*sic*] as physically more free than the reader, and thus every such book . . . is an implicit celebration of freedom."[36] Such freedom is illusory, though, because

> that incremental difference, which prevents the accomplishment of a fully synoptic closure between a sight and its seeing, is . . . engendered via the spatial and temporal displacement that is travel, an activity that eludes a proper perspective. The sight of the voyage cannot do without a voyage of the sight, since one can only take a perspective on the voyage by taking a certain distance from it, a distancing that presupposes the continuation of the voyage, the prolongation of its course.[37]

Travel writing paradoxically fixes movement over space and time. This relates both to the material content of travel writing and the metaphorical relationship between travel and writing. The frequency with which literature returns to the trope of travel suggests that this illuminates the status of literature parallel to ways of knowing more generally.[38] Both reading and writing reflect travel,[39] and the perceived distance between them can be overcome because

> the trail of the traveler obliges us to supersede the opposition be-
> tween reading and writing and to understand in its stead a complex
> circulation of signs as much written as read which modifies the
> traveler as much as he [*sic*] modifies the terrain in an endless differ-
> ential positioning, at once the infinite detour of the text and the text
> of an infinite detour.[40]

This reflexive circulation of signs means that it is impossible to move outside travel when writing or reading about it because "to talk about travel is inevitably to engage in it, to mime through the movement of one's words that which one is trying to designate with those words."[41]

According to Michel de Certeau, "every story is a travel story— a spatial practice,"[42] relating to the dialectical complexities of seeing, reading, and writing in everyday life. In this way,

> the travel story . . . does not consist of process contained and directed
> by origin and destination, nor does it oscillate between "perspectives"
> on reality. It is itself a movement organized (like any spatial story)
> between both prospective and retrospective mappings of place *and*
> the practices that transform them.[43]

To view travel and travel writing as essentially reflexive through the hermeneutic processes of reading and writing undermines perceptions of representations of an unproblematic, external "reality." To refer to the discourse of travel and its articulation through travel writing instead emphasizes the exercise of power and authority in constructions of "truth" and the associated pursuit of knowledge. I focus on travel writing by a woman in the context of late nineteenth-century British imperialism to illustrate how subject positionality was constituted differently over space, notably in terms of gender, race, and class, and how travel and travel writing were influenced and received in terms of time- and place-specific discursive formations.

IMPERIAL REPRESENTATION AND TRAVEL WRITING

Imperial travel writing is one form of textual representation informed by imperial and/or colonial discourses. In this section I destabilize imperial constructions and representations of otherness by revealing their ambivalence. I then illustrate some of the characteristics of an imperial literary tradition by referring to representations of gender and sexuality before focusing more specifically on imperial travel writing.

Colonial Discourse: Othering and Representation

According to Bhabha, the study of colonial discourse[44] should address the creation of colonial subjects, moving beyond the identification of images as positive or negative to a more profoundly structural understanding of the processes of subjectification.[45] Colonial discourse depends upon fixity in the construction of otherness, which, as "the sign of cultural/historical/racial difference," is a paradoxical form of representation, reproducing "rigidity and an unchanging order as well as disorder, degeneracy and daemonic repetition."[46] The stereotype is the main discursive codification of fixity and similarly reflects ambivalence because it "is a form of knowledge and identification that vacillates between what is always 'in place,' already known, and something that must be anxiously repeated."[47] Stereotypes do not represent false images that become discriminatory scapegoats; rather, they are ambivalent and complex in their

> projection and introjection, metaphoric and metonymic strategies, displacement, overdetermination, guilt, aggressivity; the masking and splitting of "official" and phantasmatic knowledges to construct the positionalities and oppositionalities of racist discourse.[48]

Bhabha views colonial stereotyping in terms of fetish, and he can be criticized for employing psychoanalytic categories in a potentially totalizing and ahistorical way that reproduces strategies he himself is anxious to critique.[49]

Bhabha describes ambivalence as productive, giving rise to otherness that is "an object of desire and derision, an articulation of difference contained within the fantasy of origin and identity."[50] To overlook ambivalence is to remain constrained within colonial discourse, perpetuating the hegemonic metanarrative of otherness that legitimates such a discourse. Rather than make normalizing judgments about colonial representation, we must engage with the colonial regime of "truth" that made stereotypes effective. This in turn depends upon deconstructing colonial discourse as an apparatus of power aiming to legitimate conquest over people constructed as racially inferior. To represent colonial subjects in these terms "requires an end to the collusion of historicism and realism by unseating the Transcendental subject."[51] In this way representation relates to the discursive formations and ambivalence of power, authority, "truth," and knowledge.

To "know" the colonized population legitimates discriminatory and authoritarian forms of government, as "colonization almost invariably implies a relation of structural domination and a suppression—often violent—of the heterogeneity of the subject(s) in question."[52] The colonial dialectics of seeing/knowing reflect the significance of visibility on several interdependent levels. On an ideological level, the necessity—and hence legitimation—of colonial rule is visible through, for example, notions of the "civilizing mission" and the "white man's burden";[53] and, on a more materially tangible level, the

> visibility of the institutions and apparatuses of power is possible because the exercise of colonial power makes their *relationship* obscure, produces them as fetishes, spectacles of a "natural"/racial pre-eminence.[54]

In another way visibility is maintained through the "strategies of objectification, normalisation and discipline"[55] of surveillance. But the visibility of colonial rule is itself ambivalent because to exercise authority its existence must reflect "consensual knowledge or opinion"; however, to exercise power it must represent the "objects of discrimination" beyond its control.[56] Discrimination refers to the splitting giving rise to a "colonial hybrid,"[57] whereby constructions of otherness and the visibility of colonial authority are destabilized by the recognition of differentiation:

> if the unitary (and essentialist) reference to race, nation, or cultural tradition is essential to preserve the presence of authority as an immediate mimetic effect, such essentialism must be exceeded in the articulation of "differentiatory," discriminatory identities.[58]

Edward Said's discussion of "Orientalism"[59] illuminates many of the characteristics of colonial discourse. However, in part because of his neglect of ambivalence, it may be argued that he totalizes the dichotomy between colonizing self and colonized other.[60] Orientalism relates to the production and reproduction of myths and imagined geographies constructing the inferiority of other people and places. This in turn reinforced and legitimated perceptions of Western superiority, so that the self was defined through its constructions of an other. The discourse of Orientalism is seen as composed of the changing historical and cultural relationship between Europe and Asia, the production of knowledge in the West from the early nineteenth century, and the ideological suppositions and images stimulating popular perceptions of the "Orient."[61] Three themes give coherence to these interconnected elements, namely, Said's concern with historical specificity (the alliance of Orientalism and imperialism from the eighteenth century), knowledge, and power.[62]

In resisting the totalizing metanarrative of Orientalism, Lisa Lowe has argued that multiple "orientalist situations" existed at different times and places and that each of these was internally complex, unstable, and contradictory.[63] Orientalism was one among many spatially and temporally discontinuous discourses that included "the medical and anthropological classifications of race, psychoanalytic versions of sexuality, or capitalist and Marxist constructions of class."[64] Lowe calls for the deconstruction of binary oppositions to reveal the heterogeneity of complex discursive terrains. This corresponds to feminist and postcolonial attempts, often informed by poststructuralism, to deconstruct and resist metanarratives of otherness to gain self-expression through the assertion of subjectivity. For example, all too frequently the binary opposition colonizer/colonized inhibits examination of what Spivak calls "the heterogeneity of 'Colonial Power'" at the same time that it masks the roles women play, whether [and both] as colonizers or as colonized.[65]

Overall, the powerful imperial ideology of otherness should be recognized as historically and geographically specific. Appeals to difference, whether in terms of race, gender, or class, should be contextualized and the ambivalence of such constructions revealed to avoid essentialism and the perpetuation of artificial binary oppositions.

Imperial Literary Traditions

According to Gayatri Chakravorty Spivak, two considerations are generally overlooked in readings of nineteenth-century English literature: first, imperialism was central in the cultural representation of England to the English, and second, literature stimulated such cultural self-representation.[66] By focusing largely on the emergence and importance of the English novel in the nineteenth century, Said has shown the inseparability of culture and imperialism.[67]

Imperialist literature can be seen as distinctive in the lack of contact between its object of representation and its readership, so that the "truth" of its textualization of difference was defined within wider discourses of imperial power and authority.[68] Imperialist literature represented the perceived boundaries of "civilization," but rather than explore difference, it largely affirmed its own ethnocentric perceptions:

> While the surface of each colonialist text purports to represent specific encounters with specific varieties of the racial Other, the subtext valorized the superiority of the European cultures, of the collective process that has mediated that representation.[69]

Abdul JanMohamed has contrasted "imaginary" and "symbolic" texts as two types of colonial literary representation. The former is structured by aggressive objectification through which "the subject is eclipsed by his [*sic*] fixation on and fetishization of the Other [and] the self becomes a prisoner of the projected image,"[70] while the latter seems more dialectically receptive to the potential mediation between self and other.

Before exploring the underlying characteristics of imperial travel writing and outlining my interest in travel writing by women, let me discuss representations of gender and sexuality in imperial literature generally, and travel writing more specifically, to illustrate the inherent ambivalence of imperial constructions of otherness.

Imperial Representations of Gender and Sexuality

To regard textual representations of gender and sexuality as distinctively imperial relates to imperial power and authority, the gaze, and the internal and/or external positioning in the codification of difference. It can be argued that discussing imperial literature primarily in terms of racial inequality has disguised the gender inequality experienced by both colonizing and colonized women.[71] Abena Busia writes that

> much has been said concerning the representation of the colonial native as the European "other," but as those studies done are based on texts in which [for example] African males are very much present, but scant notice is taken of the practical non-existence of African *females*, I here maintain that this analysis is strictly one of the "othering" of the African *male* as the reverse of his European counterpart. Thus, where it could be said that in the colonial novel the colonized male encounters not himself but his antithesis, the colonized woman encounters only erasure [and] sees herself only in silent spaces. The unvoicing of the black woman is literal, and her essence projected only as a void.[72]

In this account, it is notable that women are perceived as colonized rather than potential colonizers and, by extension, neglected as readers of imperial literature. Women have also been largely neglected as writers of imperial literature. Said cites women novelists throughout his account but neglects the significance of constructions of gender for both authorship and imperialism.[73] At one point he writes that

> in projecting what Raymond Williams calls a "knowable community" of Englishmen and women, Jane Austen, George Eliot, and Mrs. Gaskell shaped the idea of England in such a way as to give it identity, presence, ways of reusable articulation. And part of such an idea

was the relationship between "home" and "abroad." Thus England was surveyed, evaluated, made known, whereas "abroad" was only referred to or shown briefly without the kind of presence or immediacy lavished on London, the countryside, or northern industrial centers such as Manchester or Birmingham.[74]

Just as the imagined geographies of "abroad" were both underdeveloped and yet, in the context of imperialism, ever-present in novels, so, too, I would argue, were the imagined geographies of "home" in travel writing. In studies of imperialist novels and travel writing alike, women authors may be cited but constructions of gender are often overlooked, as illustrated by Said's reference to three women authors in the quotation above but his neglect—not only here but throughout his account—of constructions of gender difference.

By studying imperial women travel writers, I want to highlight the gendered nature of ambivalent representation on the part of women as colonizers and colonized. Considering difference constructed along lines of both gender and race reveals the complexities of labeling women as either colonizers or colonized in different contexts. However, at this stage I discuss the need to deconstruct the other by gender by focusing on the association of indigenous women with colonized land, and resulting perceptions of both feminized land and women as objects of colonization, arising from the textual articulation of sexuality in the creation of erotic as well as "exotic" spaces.

Nineteenth-century travel writers often used sexual imagery to create and sustain the heroic stature of many male explorers and travelers who wrote of conquering and penetrating dangerous, unknown continents, often characterized by the fertility of the indigenous vegetation and women.[75] Sexuality was particularly symbolic in imperial confrontation and its textual representation:

> The sex element runs as a strong undercurrent throughout [imperial literature], and the tensions induced by the strong social and moral codes are thus expressed in terms of sexual comportment, for it seems that amongst Europeans in the far-flung parts of empire, great social and political pressure manifests itself in the form of all kinds of deviant sexual behaviour. Like the colonized countries they all inhabit woman [*sic*] also becomes a subject space.[76]

This relates to Orientalist discourses, through which

> Europe was charmed by an Orient that shimmered with possibilities,
> that promised a sexual space, a voyage away from the self, an escape
> from the dictates of the bourgeois morality of the metropolis[77]

and by which the construction of a sexual domain was complemen-
tary to the construction of a domain to be colonized. However, the
sexual desire projected onto other people and places also influenced constructions of sexuality at "home" in Europe. For example,
the intermingling of constructions of racial and sexual difference
meant that there could be "a sexualization of western definitions
of these non-western societies, and an exoticization of definitions
of sexuality in European culture."[78]

Victorian patriarchy constructed women as inferior, but

> Eastern women [for example] were doubly inferior, being women
> *and* Easterners. They were an even more conspicuous commodity
> than their Western sisters. They were part of the goods of empire,
> the living rewards that white men could, if they wished to, reap.[79]

Literary representations of sexuality suggest ambivalence at the
center of imperial conquest, qualifying notions of power, authority, and legitimation. In his relationships with white women, a male
colonizer could demonstrate but not fulfill sexual mastery, as "the
woman must be ever present to be won again, and the desire for
conquest finds its own justification."[80] In contrast, colonized women
were identified with the land itself, and although miscegenation
could not be sanctioned, imperial conquest clearly did occur. Metaphors of rape emphasizing violence and the achievement of power
only through violation point to the paradoxical legitimation of
colonialism whereby

> the strategic formation of power supposedly legitimated by [impe-
> rial] texts becomes a self-betraying manoeuvre in which the supreme
> fiction is that of the deliberate usurping of the voice of the suppos-
> edly willing [indigenous] woman, rendering her falsely articulate.[81]

Nineteenth-century travel writing played an important part in
claiming authority in the vivid representation of recurrent motifs

constructing the sexuality of the other. For example, the figure of the veiled woman suggested mystery and the need for Western unveiling for comprehension, with

> this process of exposing the female Other, of literally denuding her, . . . [coming] to allegorize the Western masculinist power of possession, that she, as a metaphor for her land, becomes available for Western penetration and knowledge.[82]

A similarly vivid and common motif was that of the harem, which came to epitomize perceptions of sexual depravity and inaccessibility to the colonizer and which male writers described "with fascination and loathing."[83]

A further example of the interconnections among representations of colonial land, gender, and sexuality is the powerful mythology of Africa as the "dark continent."[84] Essentially,

> Africa grew "dark" as Victorian explorers, missionaries, and scientists flooded it with light, because the light was refracted through an imperialist ideology that urged the abolition of "savage customs" in the name of civilization.[85]

This incorporated an implicit fear and threat of falling out of the light, with such social and moral regression having powerful sexual connotations. On another level, the most graphic metaphorical expression of this can be seen in Sigmund Freud's 1926 *Essay on Lay Analysis*, in which he described the lack of knowledge concerning adult female sexuality as the "dark continent" of psychology, thus linking "the image of female sexuality to the image of the colonial black and to the perceived relationship between the female's ascribed sexuality and the Other's,"[86] and illustrating the overlaps between discourses of difference of race and gender in the totalizing conception of otherness.

Travel Writing and Imperialism

Travel writing was particularly important in imperial literary traditions because individual Europeans traveled between colonized and colonizing worlds, perpetuating mythological otherness. Individual travelers can be likened to imperial powers because

Imperialism and travel in West Africa. Courtesy of the Count de Cardi Collection, Royal Anthropological Institute.

they undertake to conquer, grasp, or assimilate challenging lands and alien peoples. They exercise the power they have (physical stamina, language ability, ingenuity, flexibility) to gain more power (knowledge of land, people, flora, fauna; knowledge of self; sense of achievement). They requisition food, shelter, carriers, and guides and return cash, medical attention, and glimpses and tokens of European culture. Like the empire, they both assert authority over and depend upon the people they encounter. Their narrative representations . . . constitute models for the national relation between Self and Other that is empire.[87]

However, to transcend totalizing discourses of self and other and thus to avoid reproducing imperialist strategies, the subjectivity of the traveler should be seen as more complex, ambiguous, and fundamentally ambivalent than implied by this dichotomization. In the case of travelers,

one recurrent feature in the as yet sketchily developed systematic study of Victorian travel narrative is an insistence on the author's

multiple persona, which allows him or her to be both accomplice
in, and critic of, the business of imperialism.[88]

In the day-to-day practice of traveling and subsequent writing, the
ideal embodiment of notions of empire in the subjectivity of the
traveler often became a critique of such a conception because of
the discursive polyphony reflecting the ambivalence of imperial
encounters and authority.

The most tangible relationship between travel and imperialism
lay in exploration and discovery, with travel writing playing
an important role in the naming and thus "owning"[89] of colonial
territories, whereby, "from the moment of this naming ritual, the
observed elements acquire significance and begin to be."[90] The
practice of naming is central to Paul Carter's conception of spatial
history as an alternative to the linear self-validation of imperial history.[91] Carter distinguishes between "discovery" and "exploration"
because

> while discovery rests on the assumption of a world of facts waiting
> to be found, collected and classified, a world in which the neutral
> observer is not implicated, exploration lays stress on the observer's
> active engagement with his [*sic*] environment: it recognizes phenom-
> ena as offspring of his intention to explore.[92]

In my discussion of women travel writers, I hope to make a further
distinction: one between travel and exploration, with travel seeming more likely to reflect self-effacing polyphony, parallel with the
gendered implications whereby women were (and continue to be)
labeled travelers—at least in a material if not a metaphorical sense—
but rarely explorers, suggesting constructions of the overt masculinity of exploration and the more passive femininity of travel. The
open-ended nature of naming seems contrary to imperial aims, but
Carter's thesis can be criticized for its reduction of such practices
to the structures of language through a focus on exclusionary structures of intentionality. While it is important to recognize the articulation of places and spaces through naming, its textuality and
intertextuality should be emphasized so that, for example, minor-
ity discourses and the gendering of discursive practices and landscape can be addressed.

Mary Louise Pratt has discussed the production of knowledge in imperial "contact zones" of transculturation from the late eighteenth century in Latin America and Africa.[93] She traces a "new planetary consciousness" characterized by interior exploration and the systematization of the natural world through Linnaean naming. Travel writing came to be informed by the distinct imperatives of "science and sentiment" that underpinned the differences between landscape narration and "manners-and-customs" ethnography: the "one produces land as landscape and territory, scanning for prospects; the other produces the indigenous inhabitants as bodyscapes, scanned also for prospects."[94] The subjectivity of the travel writer paralleled this distinction: the land-scanning, self-effacing producer of information for the state clearly differed from the sentimental experiential subject oriented more toward commerce and enterprise. Pratt argues that the paradoxical nature of observation as apparently benign yet complicit with imperialism establishes such travel writers as "anti-conquest,"[95] corresponding with notions of the ambivalence of imperial domination.

From the mid-nineteenth century, travel writing was characterized by increasingly hegemonic informational discourses aspiring to scientific status and self-legitimation, often closely allied with strategies of imperial control. Travel writing rejoined the expansion of knowledge of the natural world with the expansion of the capitalist world system, previously seen as ideologically split,[96] which suggests attempts to impose order and the interdependence of power, "truth," and knowledge within imperial discourse. But this often remained an implicit subtext in nineteenth-century travel writing, as

> to the extent that it strives to efface itself, the invisible eye/I strives to make those informational orders [aesthetic, botanical, ethnographic, ecological, and so on] natural, to find them there uncommanded, rather than assert them as the products/producers of European knowledges or disciplines. In turn, those knowledges are the producers/products of a project they likewise presuppose and seldom bespeak.[97]

Imperial travel writing varied through time and space. For example, Pratt contrasts Alexander von Humboldt's prolific writings on Latin America, describing nature in terms of the "poetics of science," with the "capitalist vanguard" from the 1820s, who expressed their concern with conquest rather than discovery in the form of linear travel accounts.[98] Perhaps the most graphic characterization of imperial travel writing, however, was the imperial discovery rhetoric of African exploration. This typically incorporated the aestheticization of landscape, the density of meaning within written texts, and clear power relations between seer and seen. According to Pratt, it was epitomized by the "monarch-of-all-I-survey" genre, which involved "particularly explicit interaction between esthetics and ideology, in what one might call a rhetoric of presence."[99]

Much Victorian traveling took place within Britain, and the motif of "social exploration" articulated class disparities, educational levels, and attempts to make sense of rapid urbanization.[100] Most often, a chronicle of a journey by upper- and middle-class writers described the working classes, mirroring constructions of self and other but highlighting the need to deconstruct and differentiate the geographies of such constructions. This also illustrates the need to be conscious of the ostensible purposes of traveling, whether at home or abroad, as well as the intended and actual readers of travel writing. Imperial travel writers were diverse in their class and occupational orientation, including, among others, "imperial explorers, merchants, professional writers of prose and poetry, anthropologists, immigrants, tourists, academics, refugees, *women and men.*"[101]

IMPERIAL TRAVEL WRITING BY WOMEN: AN INTRODUCTION

Recent interest in women travel writers has included anthologies and bibliographies;[102] descriptive and often primarily anecdotal accounts celebrating intrepid, eccentric individuals;[103] attempts to locate women travelers within the history of geography;[104] and, finally, more critical accounts exploring travel and travel writing, gendered subjectivity, imperialism, and the textualization of difference.[105] Despite this evident interest, women travelers and, more specifically, women travel writers often continue to be marginalized. For example, throughout Pratt's account of imperial travel writing, the gendered nature of travel writing is clear but not systematically discussed. Examples of women travel writers throw male travel writers into relief rather than challenge underlying notions of subjectivity. The male, heroic discourse of the capitalist vanguard in Latin America from the 1820s, emphasizing "the esthetic (or anti-esthetic) and the economic" differs from accounts by "social exploratresses" concerned with "politics and the personal."[106] Furthermore, these women travel writers were very different from the caricatured nineteenth-century phenomenon of "the Spinster Adventuress, her back to Europe, fleeing the confines of her time and returning—sometimes—to write about it."[107]

It is partly in response to such stereotypical images that Sara Mills has attempted to make women travel writers her subject of inquiry and, in so doing, to challenge and reformulate notions of subjectivity.[108] By illuminating how discourses of imperialism and of femininity articulated many often contradictory voices, she undermines individualist characterizations based on the mistaken assumption that texts by women travel writers are directly autobiographical.

To do this, Mills adopts an explicitly Foucauldian perspective, locates women within imperial discourses as producers of signification as well as signifiers, and addresses travel writing as one channel for the production of knowledge that is clearly differentiated by gender. She sees texts as part of much larger discursive formations that vary over space and time, and she views the subject positions of the women travelers themselves as inherently unstable and decentered. Yet the structure of Mills's theoretical discussion followed by three self-contained case studies seems inconsistent with such claims on epistemological and methodological grounds, and there is no indication of whether the case studies are more than arbitrary, and ultimately isolated, illustrations of her theoretical framework.[109]

To focus on individual travelers seems to replicate the strategies of imperial history in the celebration of "heroic" figures. However, their individuality should not be subsumed because, in this case in the context of nineteenth-century patriarchal discourses, each woman traveler was very much an individual. A focus on gendered subjectivity in travel writing enables the reconciliation of individuality with more general discursive formations, whether enabling or constraining in terms of textual representation.

Imperial expansion led to more opportunities for white and at least middle-class women to travel, with motives including wifely duty to husbands who were officers or officials, missionary zeal, the desire for adventure, and professional interests such as scientific research.[110] By the late nineteenth century, many women were well known for their travels, largely through their popular writings, and I focus on women travel writers to discern the gendered significance of their writings as well as their travels. The form of travel writing can be seen as gendered, with goal-oriented "quest romances" and "tragedies," in which similar goals are set but not fulfilled, constructed as masculine and "odysseys," referring to travel for its own sake, constructed as feminine.[111] The conventions and constraints shaping travel writing are clearly gendered. For example, the role of heroic adventurer was available to a male narrator, but women were constrained by feminine codes of conduct. In terms of sexual imagery, women were more likely to be self-effacing, developing strategies of accommodation rather than confrontation and emphasizing their femininity. Another general difference relates to claims for scientific accuracy and professionalism, with scientifically oriented male exploration contrasting again with the more self-conscious tone of many women travel writers in the perceived need to vouch for scientific accuracy.[112]

Women travel writers described their experiences of moving both within and between patriarchal and imperial discourses that were spatially differentiated in their influences. It was in centers of colonial settlement that the intermingling of patriarchal and imperial discourses stimulated, for example, the greatest questioning of the single status of many women travelers in the nineteenth century.[113] However, once the travelers were beyond the confinement of European colonial society, imperial discourses of power and structural inequality arguably came to supersede those of patriarchal discourses, and women travelers became increasingly able to share in the authority of male colonizers. Mills argues that racial status constructed by colonial discourses of difference overcame the gender inferiority created by patriarchal discourses of difference.[114]

I want to show that a discursive interpretation of travel and travel writing can reveal the spatiality of both discourse and travel.[115] In grounding such a discursive interpretation, I need to position Mary Kingsley's travels and travel writing within the broader contexts of travel and imperialism. I emphasize notions of ambivalence to undermine the dichotomization of a colonial self and colonized other. It is important to recognize constructions of subjectivity along lines of gender, race, and class to deconstruct totalizing notions of difference because

> the intersection of colonial and gender discourses involves a shifting, contradictory subject positioning, whereby Western women can simultaneously constitute "centre" and "periphery," identity and alterity. A Western woman, in these narratives, exists in a relation of subordination to Western man and in a relation of domination toward "non-Western" men and women.[116]

CONCLUSION

Studying women travel writers of the late nineteenth century poses both substantive and theoretical challenges. It is important to be aware of the significance of travel and travel writing, the distinctive nature of imperial representation, and how both travel writing and imperial representation more broadly were differentiated by constructions of gender. Nineteenth-century British travel writing offers the greatest potential for such a study because of the hegemony of imperial power relations, graphically constructing and legitimating a colonized other. However, rather than replicate imperial discourses, it is important to give voice to those marginalized by such totalizations while at the same time revealing their ambivalence rather than fixity. This involves sensitivity to constructions of difference along lines of gender, race, and class, which are inextricably intertwined in the constitution and contestation of subjectivity. I focus on Kingsley to illuminate the spatial differentiation of patriarchy and imperialism, and the textual representation of such differentiation. In this way, I seek to expose the relationships among subjectivity, power, authority, constructions of "truth," and the associated production of knowledge, informed by the claim that

> a working alliance may be formed between *deconstruction*, as a process of displacement which registers an attempted dissociation from a dominant discursive system or systems, and *decolonization* as a

process of cultural transformation which involves the ongoing critique of colonial discourse.[117]

The imperatives of deconstruction and decolonization relate to the need to perceive subjectivity as discursively constructed and to expose the instability of constructions of "home" and "truth" as material and metaphorical reference points. In the case of women travel writers, I want to show how the ambivalence of these constructions exposed and challenged the ideology of otherness, particularly in perceptions of race and gender over space and time.

NOTES

1. The term "metaphor" originates from the Greek *metaphorein*, meaning to transfer or transport; see G. Van den Abbeele, *Travel as Metaphor: From Montaigne to Rousseau* (Minneapolis: University of Minnesota Press, 1992).

2. See, for example, b. hooks, *Yearning: Race, Gender and Cultural Politics* (Boston: South End Press, 1990). For critiques and commentaries on spatial metaphors by geographers, see L. Bondi and M. Domosh, "Other Figures in Other Places: On Feminism, Postmodernism and Geography," *Environment and Planning D: Society and Space* 10 (1992): 199–213; S. Pile and G. Rose, "All or Nothing? Politics and Critique in the Modernism-Postmodernism Debate," *Environment and Planning D: Society and Space* 10 (1992): 123–136; and G. Pratt, "Commentary: Spatial Metaphors and Speaking Positions," *Environment and Planning D: Society and Space* 10 (1992): 241–244. Pratt identifies three sets of spatial metaphors in current use: those drawing on the rhetoric of mobility, those emphasizing marginality and exile, and those representing the borderland as a place.

3. J. Wolff, "On the Road Again: Metaphors of Travel in Cultural Criticism," *Cultural Studies* 7 (1993): 224–239. She traces three origins of travel vocabularies, namely, postcolonialism, postmodernism, and poststructuralism.

4. E. W. Said, *The World, the Text, and the Critic* (Cambridge, MA: Harvard University Press, 1983).

5. J. Clifford, "Traveling Cultures," in *Cultural Studies*, ed. L. Grossberg, C. Nelson, and P. Treichler (London: Routledge, 1992).

6. Clifford 1992, 110.

7. See, for example, bell hooks's critique of Clifford in which she states: "From certain standpoints, to travel is to encounter the terrorizing force of white supremacy." b. hooks, "Representing Whiteness in the Black Imagination," in Grossberg et al., 1992, 344.

8. C. Kaplan, "Deterritorializations: The Rewriting of Home and Exile in Western Feminist Discourse," *Cultural Critique* 6 (Spring 1987): 187–198; p. 191.

9. Van den Abbeele 1992, xxiii.

10. Ibid., xviii–xix.

11. Ibid., xix.

12. Ibid., 47.

13. Ibid., 50.

14. Wolff 1993, 224.

15. M. Morris, "At Henry Parkes Motel," *Cultural Studies* 2, 1 (1988): 1–16 and 29–47. Morris criticizes Van den Abbeele's earlier work in this article, particularly G. Van den Abbeele, "Sightseers: The Tourist as Theorist," *Diacritics*, 10 (1980): 2–14.

16. See M. B. Pratt, "Identity: Skin Blood Heart," in *Yours in Struggle*, ed. E. Burkin, M. B. Pratt, and B. Smith (Ithaca, NY: Firebrand Books, 1984), in which she discusses different meanings of "home" inscribed in space. Also see B. Martin and C. T. Mohanty, "Feminist Politics: What's Home Got to Do with It?" in *Feminist Studies/Critical Studies*, ed. T. de Lauretis (Bloomington: Indiana University Press, 1986).

17. Van den Abbeele 1992. For more on the Enlightenment, see G. Lloyd, *The Man of Reason: "Male" and "Female" in Western Philosophy* (London: Methuen, 1984). For further discussion on the masculinity of the gaze, which arguably gained preeminence from the Enlightenment, see, for example, M. A. Doane, *The Desire to Desire* (Bloomington: Indiana University Press, 1987); L. Mulvey, *Visual and Other Pleasures* (Basingstoke, England: Macmillan, 1989); G. Pollock, *Vision and Difference: Femininity, Feminism and Histories of Art* (London: Routledge, 1988); G. Rose, "Geography as a Science of Observation: The Landscape, the Gaze and Masculinity," in *Nature and Science: Essays in the History of Geographical Knowledge*, ed. F. Driver and G. Rose (London: Historical Geography Research Group of the Institute of British Geographers, 1992); and J. Rose, *Sexuality in the Field of Vision* (London: Verso, 1986).

18. R. Radhakrishnan, "Feminist Historiography and Post-structuralist Thought," in *The Difference within: Feminism and Critical Theory*, ed. E. Meese and A. Parker (Amsterdam: John Benjamins, 1989), 195.

19. E. W. Said, *Culture and Imperialism* (New York: Alfred A. Knopf, 1993), 332. My emphasis.

20. H. K. Bhabha, "The World and the Home," *Social Text* 31/32 (1992): 141–153.

21. R. Marangoly George, "Traveling Light: Of Immigration, Invisible Suitcases, and Gunny Sacks," *Differences* 4, 2 (1992): 72–99; p. 72.

22. P. Carter, *Living in a New Country: History, Travelling and Language* (London: Faber and Faber, 1992), 101.

23. P. Fussell, *Abroad: British Literary Traveling between the Wars* (New York: Oxford University Press, 1980), 38.

24. Fussell 1980, 39.

25. J. Urry, *The Tourist Gaze: Leisure and Travel in Contemporary Societies* (London: Sage, 1990).

26. Urry's consideration of the gazing subject seems largely limited to constructions of class difference. Gender and race are textually as well

as substantively peripheral, receiving inadequate commentary at the end of the book.

27. H. K. Bhabha, "Articulating the Archaic: Notes on Colonial Nonsense," In *Literary Theory Today*, ed. P. Collier and H. Geyer-Ryan (Ithaca, NY: Cornell University Press, 1990), 205.

28. J. Culler, *Framing the Sign: Criticism and Its Institutions* (Norman: University of Oklahoma Press, 1988), 159.

29. Ibid., 160, following D. MacCannell, *The Tourist* (New York: Schocken, 1976).

30. Ibid., 164.

31. I. S. MacLaren, "Introduction," *Ariel* 21, 4 (October 1990): 6. For discussion of the historical background and significance of travel writing, see, for example, P. Adams, *Travel Literature and the Evolution of the Novel* (Lexington: University Press of Kentucky, 1983); C. Batten, *Pleasurable Instruction: Form and Convention in Eighteenth Century Travel Literature* (Berkeley: University of California Press, 1978); and M. Campbell, *The Witness and the Other World: Exotic European Travel Writing, 400–1600* (Ithaca, NY: Cornell University Press, 1988).

32. M. Van Wyk Smith, "'Arbitrary Rule' and the Eighteenth Century Discourse of Guinea," *Ariel* 21, 4 (October 1990): 119–137.

33. A. Hassam, "'As I Write': Narrative Occasions and the Quest for Self-Presence in the Travel Diary," *Ariel* 21, 4 (October 1990): 33–47; p. 41.

34. S. Blake, "Travel and Literature: The Liberian Narratives of Esther Warner and Graham Greene," *Research in African Literature* 22, 2 (1991): 191–203; p. 192.

35. Van den Abbeele 1992. See Chapter 2, this volume, for further discussion of authorial authority and its implications for notions of gendered subjectivity.

36. Fussell 1980, 203.

37. Van den Abbeele 1992, 71–72.

38. Ibid. Also see J. Stratton, *Writing Sites: A Genealogy of the Postmodern World* (London: Harvester Wheatsheaf, 1990). He writes that "writing, the representational site of knowledge, provides the space within which travel occurs. In a world which is constituted as the space of writing, knowledge is able to travel" (p. 56).

39. See, for example, Fussell 1980, who states that, first, "in reading, of all books, a travel book, the reader becomes doubly a traveler, moving from beginning to end of the book while touring along with the literary traveler" (p. 211); and, second, that "writing . . . is like traveling. Figures of travel occupy any writer's imagination as he [*sic*] starts out, makes transitions, digresses, returns, goes forward, divagates, pauses, approaches the subject from a slightly different direction, and observes things from a different point of view" (pp. 211–212).

40. Van den Abbeele 1992, 7–8.

41. Ibid., xxx.

42. M. de Certeau, *The Practice of Everyday Life*, trans. S. Randall (Berkeley: University of California Press, 1984), 115.

43. Morris 1988, 38.

44. Following Said 1993, I use "imperialism" to mean "the practice, the theory, and the attitudes of a dominating metropolitan center ruling a distant territory; 'colonialism,' which is almost always a consequence of imperialism, is the implanting of settlements on distant territory" (p. 9). Said later states that "modern European imperialism was a constitutively, radically different type of overseas domination from all earlier forms" (p. 221) because of its scale, longevity, and the massive organization of imperial power. I want neither to privilege "imperialism" or "colonialism" nor to perceive them as mutually exclusive. I refer to women travel writers of this period—specifically Kingsley—as imperial because the places they traveled through were under imperial but not necessarily colonial control. This also reflects that they themselves were moving rather than fixed in colonial settlements, and also that they often passed through areas under the imperial influence of different imperial, but not necessarily colonial, powers. However, at this stage I am referring to "colonial discourse" because I am discussing Bhabha's work employing this term.

45. H. K. Bhabha, "The Other Question . . . ," *Screen* 24, 6 (1983): 18–36.

46. Ibid., 18.

47. Ibid.

48. Ibid., 34.

49. See, for example, R. Young, *White Mythologies : Writing History and the West* (London: Routledge, 1990). For further critiques, see B. Parry, "Problems in Current Theories of Colonial Discourse," *Oxford Literary Review* 9 (1987): 27–58; and A. Loomba, "Overworlding the 'Third World,'" *Oxford Literary Review* 13 (1991): 164–191.

50. Bhabha 1983, 19.

51. H. K. Bhabha, "Representation and the Colonial Text : A Critical Exploration of Some Forms of Mimeticism," in *The Theory of Reading*, ed. F. Gloversmith (Brighton, England: Harvester Press, 1984), 98.

52. C. T. Mohanty, "Under Western Eyes: Feminist Scholarship and Colonial Discourses," *Boundary* 2, 3 (1984): 333–358; p. 333.

53. These are referred to as "moralistic and normative ideologies of amelioration" by Bhabha 1983, 35.

54. Ibid. In addition, see T. Mitchell, *Colonizing Egypt* (Cambridge, England: Cambridge University Press, 1988), for discussion of how the exercise of colonial power and authority were inscribed in space.

55. Bhabha 1983, 35.

56. H. K. Bhabha, "Signs Taken for Wonders : Questions of Ambivalence and Authority under a Tree Outside Delhi, May 1817," *Critical Inquiry* 12 (Autumn 1985): 144–165; p. 154.

57. Ibid.

58. Ibid., 154.

59. E. W. Said, *Orientalism* (New York: Vintage Books, 1979).

60. As argued by, for example, F. Driver, "Geography's Empire: Histories of Geographical Knowledge," *Environment and Planning D: Society and Space* 10 (1992): 23–40; and L. Lowe, *Critical Terrains: French and British Orientalisms* (Ithaca, NY: Cornell University Press, 1991).

61. E. W. Said, "Orientalism Reconsidered," *Cultural Critique* 1 (Fall 1985): 89–107.

62. L. Mani and R. Frankenberg, "The Challenge of Orientalism," *Economy and Society* 14, 2 (May 1985): 174–192.

63. Lowe 1991, 5.

64. Ibid., 8.

65. C. A. Holmlund, "Displacing Limits of Difference: Gender, Race, and Colonialism in Edward Said and Homi Bhabha's Theoretical Models and Marguerite Duras's Experimental Films," *Quarterly Review of Film and Video* 13 (1991): 1–22.

66. G. C. Spivak, "Three Women's Texts and a Critique of Imperialism," *Critical Inquiry* 12 (Autumn 1985): 243–261.

67. Said 1993. Said states that "the novel, as a cultural artifact of bourgeois society, and imperialism are unthinkable without each other. . . . Imperialism and the novel fortified each other to such a degree that it is impossible, I would argue, to read one without in some way dealing with the other" (pp. 70–71).

68. A. R. JanMohamed, "The Economy of Manichean Allegory: The Function of Racial Difference in Colonialist Literature," *Critical Inquiry* 12 (Autumn 1985): 59–87.

69. Ibid., 65.

70. Ibid., 67.

71. A. P. A. Busia, "Miscegenation as Metonymy: Sexuality and Power in the Colonial Novel," *Ethnic and Racial Studies* 9 (1986): 360–372; p. 362.

72. Ibid., 369.

73. Said 1993. I discuss the gendered significance of authorship and authority in Chapter 2.

74. Ibid., 72.

75. See, for example, Said 1985, Busia 1986, and K. Schaffer, *Women and the Bush: Forces of Desire in the Australian Cultural Tradition* (Cambridge, England: Cambridge University Press, 1990).

76. Busia 1986, 363.

77. R. Kabbani, *Europe's Myths of Orient : Devise and Rule* (London: Macmillan, 1986), 67.

78. J. De Groot, "'Sex' and 'Race': The Construction of Language and Image in the Nineteenth Century," in *Sexuality and Subordination: Interdisciplinary Studies of Gender in the Nineteenth Century*, ed. S. Mendus and J. Rendall (London: Routledge, 1989), 100.

79. Kabbani 1986, 51.

80. Busia 1986, 370.

81. Ibid., 371.

82. E. Shohat, "Gender and Culture of Empire: Toward a Feminist Ethnography of the Cinema," *Quarterly Review of Film and Video* 13 (1991): 45-84; p. 57. Also see De Groot 1989.

83. L. Ahmed, "Western Ethnocentrism and Perceptions of the Harem," *Feminist Studies* 8, 3 (1982): 521-534; p. 524. See also *Half-veiled Truths: Western Travellers' Perceptions of Middle Eastern Women*, ed. J. Mabro (London: I. B. Tauris, 1991); and B. Melman, *Women's Orients: English Women and the Middle East, 1718-1918: Sexuality, Religion and Work* (London: Macmillan, 1992). Melman describes a distinctively feminine tradition of harem literature characterized by familiarity and domesticity.

84. See the Interlude for further discussion of how the myth of the "dark continent" informed imagined geographies of Africa in the nineteenth century.

85. P. Brantlinger, "Victorians and Africans: The Genealogy of the Myth of the Dark Continent," *Critical Inquiry* 12 (Autumn 1985): 166-203; p. 166.

86. S. L. Gilman, "Black Bodies, White Bodies: Toward an Iconography of Female Sexuality in Late Nineteenth Century Art, Medicine, and Literature," *Critical Inquiry* 12 (Autumn 1985): 204-242; p. 238.

87. S. L. Blake, "A Woman's Trek: What Difference Does Gender Make?" *Women's Studies International Forum* 13, 4 (1990): 347-355; p. 348.

88. E.-M. Kroller, "First Impressions: Rhetorical Strategies in Travel Writing by Victorian Women," *Ariel* 21, 4 (October 1990): 87-99; p. 87.

89. M. Blythe, "'What's in a Name?' Film Culture and the Self/Other Question," *Quarterly Review of Film and Video* 13 (1991): 205-215.

90. Kabbani 1986, 86.

91. P. Carter, *The Road to Botany Bay: An Essay in Spatial History* (London: Faber and Faber, 1987).

92. Carter 1987, 25.

93. M. L. Pratt, *Imperial Eyes: Travel Writing and Transculturation* (London: Routledge, 1992).

94. Ibid., 64.

95. Ibid.

96. M. L. Pratt, "Scratches on the Face of the Country; or, What Mr Barrow Saw in the Land of the Bushmen," *Critical Inquiry* 12 (Autumn 1985): 119-143. This essay is reprinted in part in M. L. Pratt 1992.

97. M. L. Pratt 1992, 125.

98. Ibid. Pratt illustrates the relational nature of transculturation by showing how Humboldt's work and identity influenced Creole self-fashioning by contributing toward an elite and powerful official culture.

99. Ibid., 205. See Chapter 4, this volume, for further discussion.

100. J. Shattock, "Travel Writing Victorian and Modern: A Review of Recent Research," in *The Art of Travel: Essays on Travel Writing*, ed. P. Dodd (London: Frank Cass, 1982).

101. MacLaren 1990, 6. My emphasis.

102. See, for example, *Ladies on the Loose: Women Travellers of the Eighteenth and Nineteenth Centuries*, ed. L. Hamalian (New York: Dodd and Mead, 1981); J. Robinson, *Wayward Women: A Guide to Women Travellers* (Oxford, England: Oxford University Press, 1990); and M. Tinling, *Women into the Unknown: A Sourcebook of Women Explorers and Travellers* (New York: Greenwood Press, 1989).

103. Including A. Allen, *Travelling Ladies* (London: Jupiter,1980); D. Middleton, *Victorian Lady Travellers* (London: Routledge and Kegan Paul, 1965); M. Russell, *The Blessings of a Good Thick Skirt: Women Travellers and Their World* (London: Collins, 1988); and C. Stevenson, *Victorian Women Travel Writers in Africa* (Boston: Twayne, 1982).

104. D. Middleton, "Some Victorian Lady Travellers," *Geographical Journal* 139 (1973): 65–75. For more recent interest, see M. Domosh, "Toward a Feminist Historiography of Geography," *Transactions of the Institute of British Geographers* N.S. 16 (1991a): 95–104; M. Domosh, "Beyond the Frontiers of Geographical Knowledge," *Transactions of the Institute of British Geographers* N.S. 16 (1991b): 488–490; and D. R. Stoddart, "Do We Need a Feminist Historiography of Geography—and if We Do, What Should It Be?" *Transactions of the Institute of British Geographers* N.S. 16 (1991): 484–487; as discussed in the Introduction.

105. See, for example, D. Birkett, *Spinsters Abroad: Victorian Lady Explorers* (Oxford, England: Basil Blackwell, 1989); Blake 1990; Kroller 1990; N. Kyle, "Cara David and the 'Truths' of Her 'Unscientific' Travellers' Tales in Australia and the South Pacific," *Women's Studies International Forum* 16, 2 (1993): 105–118; Melman 1992; S. Mills, "Discourses of Difference," *Cultural Studies* 4, 2 (1990): 128–140; S. Mills, *Discourses of Difference: An Analysis of Women's Travel Writing and Colonialism* (London: Routledge, 1991); and S. Morgan, "An Introduction to Victorian Women's Travel Writings about Southeast Asia," *Genre* 20 (1987): 189–208.

106. M. L. Pratt 1992, 168.

107. Ibid., 171.

108. Although her earlier work reflects these concerns, too, I am particularly referring to Mills 1991.

109. The case studies—all from the "high imperialist" period of the mid-nineteenth to the early twentieth centuries—would be more effective if integrated within Mills's theoretical parameters, and with each other, in a reflexively self-conscious way. Attempts to expose a text written by Alexandra David-Neel as fabrication illustrate how texts written by women travel writers have been judged as a whole; the conflicting coexistence of colonial, feminine, and masculine voices within Kingsley's *Travels in West Africa* is facilitated by humor, irony, and parody that destabilize preconceptions of a fixed, authoritative narrator; and, finally, the less well known writings of Nina Mazuchelli seem firmly rooted within feminine discourses but are shown as similarly constrained within colonial discourses of difference.

110. Robinson 1990.

111. Stevenson 1982.

112. Birkett 1989.

113. Ibid.

114. Mills 1990.

115. See, for example, Lowe 1991, and S. Hutchinson, *Cervantine Journeys* (Madison: University of Wisconsin Press,1992).

116. Shohat 1991, 63.

117. G. Huggan, "Maps and Mapping Strategies in Contemporary Canadian and Australian Fiction" (Ph.D. thesis, University of British Columbia, 1989), 248.

(Re)presenting
Mary Kingsley

Mary Kingsley played many roles throughout her brief life—dutiful daughter, loyal sister, fearless traveler, well-known author and public speaker, political lobbyist, and wartime nurse. These roles were spatially distinct, with Kingsley moving from the domestic, familial sphere of home to gain individual independence while traveling. "Home" changed dramatically on Kingsley's return. She mediated private and public spheres of activity by coexisting as housekeeper for her brother and as a prominent, controversial political figure advocating trade in West Africa.

I focus on Kingsley because her life vividly illustrates attempts to balance a sense of duty with the desire for independence, because she traveled to West Africa rather than all over the world, because she wrote two books about her travels, and because she was an outspoken figure in imperial debates of the 1890s. There is also a wealth of archival material on Kingsley, including her publications, articles, letters, reviews and obituaries in national and regional newspapers, and her letters to, among others, her publisher, George Macmillan, and the trader John Holt.[1]

Mary Henrietta Kingsley was born in 1862 in Islington, North London.[2] Her family was a well-known literary one: her uncle Charles Kingsley was the author of *Westward Ho!* and *The Water Babies*, and her cousin, also called Mary, was better known as the novelist Lucas Malet. Mary's father, George, was a doctor who traveled widely as the personal physician to titled and wealthy men, returning to Britain for a few months every year or so. From 1862 to the early 1890s, he traveled in Spain, Egypt, Syria, North Africa,

North America, and the South Pacific. Three weeks before sailing for the Mediterranean, on October 9, 1862, George married Mary Bailey, whom he had employed in a domestic capacity. Mary Kingsley was born four days later. Her brother Charles was born in 1866, and in the following year George embarked on his longest and most distant journey, spending three years in the South Pacific with the earl of Pembroke.

Kingsley's account of her childhood suggests her isolation within the familial sphere, able only to read about an outside world:

> The whole of my childhood and youth was spent at home, in the house and garden. The living outside world I saw little of, and cared less for, for I felt myself out of place at the few parties I ever had the chance of going to, and I deservedly was unpopular with my own generation, for I knew nothing of play and such things. But this was not a superiority of mind in me, at all, the truth was I had a great amusing world of my own other people did not know, or care about—that was in the books in my father's library.[3]

She cited her favorite books as Burton's *Anatomy of Melancholy*, Johnson's *Robberies and Murders of the Most Notorious Pyrates*, Bayle's *Dictionary*, and Lockyer's *Solar Physics*, suggesting a serious, studious, and lonely determination to educate herself.[4] Her dependence on such books is vividly evident in her comment that "what the *English Mechanic* was to me for years I cannot explain. What I should have done without its companionship between 16 and 20 I do not care to think."[5] As well as seeming isolated from "the living outside world," Kingsley also seems to have been isolated within the sphere of family life: "My home authorities said I had no business to want to be taught such things, but presented me with a copy of Craik's *Pursuit of Knowledge Under Difficulties*."[6]

While George Kingsley traveled, his wife suffered increasingly bad health at home and was largely cared for by Mary. In 1884 the family moved to Cambridge, where Charles attended Christ's College. In a letter to George Macmillan of 1899, Mary compared the amount of money spent on her brother's formal education with that spent on hers, which was purely oriented to being her father's research assistant:

> I do not know if I ever revealed to you that being allowed to learn German was *all* the paid for education I ever had—two thousand pounds was spent on my brother—I still hope not in vain.[7]

Mary Kingsley's earliest travels were constrained by her domestic role. She first traveled away from home when she was 25, staying in Wales. However, she had to return home after two days because of a relapse in her mother's condition. The following year she spent a week in Paris, but on her return her mother suffered a further relapse, which meant that Mary was unable to leave home for more than several hours at a time. She studied classical and Syrian Arabic and continued her wide reading on travel, anthropology, and the physical sciences. Mary was more restricted within the domestic sphere than ever before, and she described this period as

> years of work and watching and anxiety, a narrower life in home interests than ever, and a more hopelessly depressing one, for it was a long losing fight with death all the time.[8]

Her father returned from his last journey and died in February 1892, and her mother died in April of the same year. When Charles left for the Far East in June, Mary traveled to the Canary Islands and came into her first contact with West Coast traders. When she returned to Britain, Mary moved to London with her brother, and whenever he was in the country, she kept house for him. As she states in the opening sentence of *Travels in West Africa*, "It was in 1893 that, for the first time in my life, I found myself in possession of five or six months which were not heavily forestalled."[9]

Mary Kingsley made two journeys to West Africa, from August 1893 to early January 1894, and from December 1894 to November 1895. As shown in the map of territories and advances of imperial powers in West Africa, Britain, France, Germany, Portugal, and Spain had influence in this region. Imagined geographies of Africa in Britain at this time were most vividly articulated as images of a "dark continent." The construction of this liminal space was inseparable from imperialism because

> by the 1860s the success of the antislavery movement, the impact of the great Victorian explorers, and the merger in the social sciences of racist and evolutionary doctrines had combined, and the public widely shared a view of Africa which demanded imperialization on moral, religious, and scientific grounds.[10]

The sensationalist mythology of Africa as a "dark continent" was a Victorian invention that was both created by and also helped

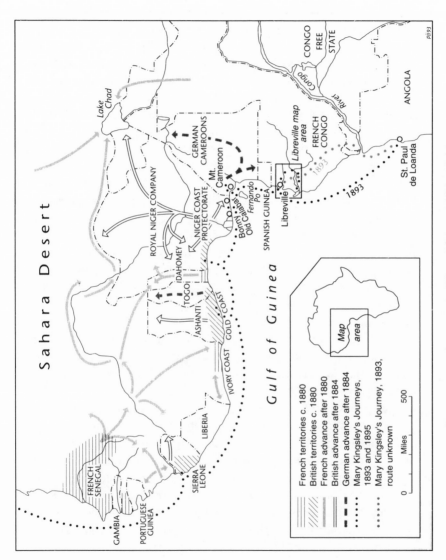

European advances in West Africa, 1880–1900.

to create a growing imperial monopoly on discourse. Displacing blame for the slave trade onto Africans

> fused with sensational reports about cannibalism, witchcraft, and apparently shameless sexual customs to drape Victorian Africa in that pall of darkness which Victorians themselves accepted as reality.[11]

After the 1870s, exploration had largely given way to commercial exploitation through trade. The "new imperialism" of the late nineteenth century "was viewed as a panacea for some of the economic ills of the time as well as providing apparently limitless opportunities for missionary endeavour, scientific study, settlement and commercial enterprise."[12] At this time jingoism celebrated overseas expansion, which was seen as necessary for the survival of capitalism in England.[13] Thomas Richards has described the importance of Victorian commodity culture to imperialism and, specifically, to images of "darkest Africa." Commodities came to be transformed from instruments of trade to those of expansionist policy. Ultimately, however, the exchange of commodities transcended national spheres of influence, potentially superseding expansionist policy: "The commodity form makes distribution placeless, for once the commodity has been established as the form of exchange, exchange can take place anywhere."[14]

In light of this, it is significant that Kingsley traded to pay her way, and that she traveled and traded largely in areas under French and German administrative but not necessarily commercial control.[15] In West Africa by the late nineteenth century, Europeans had established trading agencies to buy ivory, timber, rubber, and palm oil. Kingsley traveled most extensively in Gabon, where, despite its formal annexation to the French Congo since 1890, Britain was more commercially successful through trade, particularly along the Ogowé River.[16] The two main British companies, John Holt and Hatton and Cookson, benefited from the strength of British industry, steamship lines that ran to West Africa well in advance of trade, and the financial advantages of being larger than their smaller French counterparts.[17]

In contrast to many African explorations, Kingsley traveled on a modest scale, either alone or with small groups of Africans. On her first journey, she called in at Freetown, Cape Coast, Accra, the Bight of Benin, Bonny, and St. Paul do Loanda. For the next four

Mary Kingsley sitting between Sir Claude and Lady Rose MacDonald in Calabar, 1895. Courtesy of the Royal Commonwealth Society Library, London.

months she journeyed inland and north through Cabinda, the Congo Free State, French Congo, and Cameroon until she reached Calabar, from where she sailed home. This trip seems to have been very much like a reconnaissance journey to prepare for future travels. When she returned to West Africa, Kingsley was equipped with a collector's outfit from the British Museum—which included bottles and 15 gallons of spirit[18]—and claimed to be studying "fish and fetish." Again she traveled via Sierra Leone, the Cape Coast, and

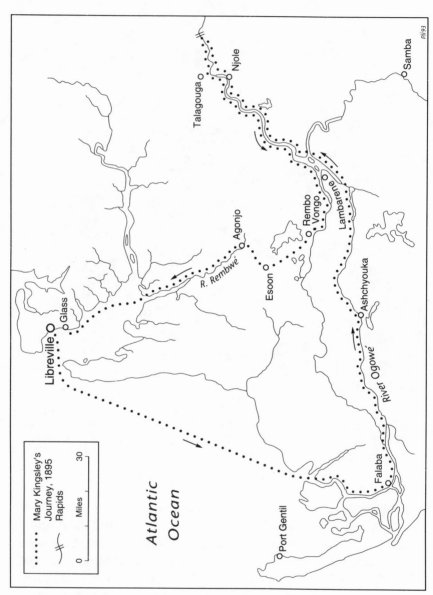

Mary Kingsley's route, 1895. Adapted from Kingsley, Travels in West Africa (1897).

Atlantic
Ocean

Mary Kingsley's
Journey, 1895
Rapids

Miles
0   30

Libreville
Glass
Port Gentil
R. Rembwé
Agonjo
Esoon
Rembo
Vongo
Lambarene
Ashchyouka
River Ogowé
Falaba
Talagouga
Njole
Samba

JOURNAL OF THE
AFRICAN SOCIETY

FOUNDED IN MEMORY OF
MARY KINGSLEY

Title page of the Journal of the African Society. *Courtesy of the Royal African Society, London. The title page remained the same until volume 23 in 1923/1924, when the emblem of Mary Kingsley was changed to an image of Africa.*

the Gold Coast, but this time only as far as Calabar and in the company of Lady MacDonald, the wife of the governor of the British Niger Coast Protectorate. Kingsley traveled to Fernando Po with the MacDonalds, and in May landed at the port of Glass. From there she set off for the Ogowé River (see the map of her route), going over the rapids and through the bush in the company of Fans, infamous for their cannibalism. Her final expedition was climbing Mount Cameroon by a route previously untraveled by Europeans.

Kingsley returned home with 65 species of fish and 18 species of reptile, and three new species of fish were named after her. She hoped to remain in Britain for no longer than a year, but personal and political demands kept her there until 1900. Kingsley published two books about her travels: *Travels in West Africa* in 1897 and *West African Studies* in 1899.[19] The first is more descriptive about her travels, while the second includes her alternative plan for the government of West Africa. Kingsley's controversial opinions were all underpinned by her support for trade in West Africa and, specifically, the Liverpool trading lobby. She criticized colonial administration, arguing that it was necessary to understand indigenous customs and that traders should have greatest influence over policy. She also criticized missionaries, supported the liquor trade, and attempted to place taboo subjects such as polygamy and cannibalism in their African contexts.

Kingsley's final journey to Africa was to the south to nurse Boer prisoners of war. She contracted typhoid and died on June 3, 1900, at the age of 37.[20] She was buried at sea with both naval and military honors. The most tangible memorial to her was the foundation of the African Society, now the Royal African Society.

According to Kingsley,

> My life can be written in a very few lines. It is, and has been, and will be, one wholly without romance or variety in the proper sense of the word; it has just been one long grind of work, work worth doing, but never well done, and never successful in gaining the thing aimed at, a perpetual Waterloo in a microscopic way. Why this has been is perfectly clear; it arises from my having no personal individuality of my own whatsoever. I have always lived in the lives of other people, whose work was heavy for them; and, apart from that, I have lived a life of my own, strewn about among non-human things; but I doubt, even if an energetic individual were to go round with a broom and sweep the universe for me, that sufficient could be got together to be called a personality.[21]

Kingsley's overwhelmingly melancholic tone stands in stark contrast to the remarkable life and vivid personality that emerge in her own and others' writings about her life and travels. Rather than celebrate and individualize her achievements, I want to reveal their significance in broader discursive terms, in particularly focusing on how Kingsley negotiated "home" and away, private and public spheres, as a woman in the context of British imperialism in the 1890s. Overall, I illustrate how discourses of gender, race, and class constructed the patriarchal and imperial discourses shaping and constraining subjectivity over space and time.

NOTES

1. See the first section of the bibliography for complete archival references.

2. The first biography of Mary Kingsley—first published in 1932—was S. Gwynn, *The Life of Mary Kingsley* (Harmondsworth: Penguin, 1940), which contains many extracts from Kingsley's correspondence. This was

followed by O. Campbell, *Mary Kingsley: A Victorian in the Jungle* (London: Methuen, 1957). Since then, Kingsley has been described in fictionalized accounts, in children's books, and in virtually all of the accounts of women travel writers cited in Chapter 1. The most detailed biographies are D. Birkett, *Mary Kingsley—Imperial Adventuress* (London: Macmillan, 1992); and K. Frank, *A Voyager Out: The Life of Mary Kingsley* (Boston: Houghton Mifflin, 1986a). Another recent biography is R. D. Pearce, *Mary Kingsley: Light at the Heart of Darkness* (Oxford, England: Kensal, 1990). Also see C. Alexander, *One Dry Season: In the Footsteps of Mary Kingsley* (New York: Vintage, 1991), for a contemporary travel account by a woman following Mary Kingsley's route in Gabon.

3. M. H. Kingsley, "In the Days of My Youth," *Mainly about People* (May 20, 1899a): 468–469.

4. Ibid.

5. Ibid.

6. Ibid.

7. Mary Kingsley to George Macmillan (undated, January 1899). In other letters to Macmillan, Kingsley's concern and impatience with her brother, prompted by his lack of employment, his ill health, and his tardiness and lack of commitment to producing the memoir of their father, become prominent. For example, in a letter of August 14, 1896, Kingsley wrote that "it makes me very unhappy about him because this disinclination of his to grind at anything but abstract metaphysics coupled with house property at Bexley Heath, cannot lead to Fortune—and he is not like me indifferent to creature comforts." Regarding his ill health, Kingsley wrote to Macmillan on April 2, 1897, that "Charley does not seem better but says he is. I cannot work when I am as worried as I am just now about him." Finally, Kingsley referred to his inactivity in compiling their father's memoir; on June 18, 1896, she stated, "I have had no talk with Charley yet about the memoir but I have reason to think I was wrong and he has *not* burnt it," and in her letter of February 23, 1897, she wrote that "Charley is showing signs of life over the memoir."

8. Kingsley 1899a.

9. M. H. Kingsley, *Travels in West Africa: Congo Français, Corisco and Cameroons*, 5th ed. (London: Virago, 1986), 1. This was first published in 1897 by Macmillan, London.

10. P. Brantlinger, *Rule of Darkness: British Literature and Imperialism, 1830–1914* (Ithaca, NY: Cornell University Press, 1988), 174.

11. Brantlinger 1988, 196.

12. J. MacKenzie "Geography and Imperialism: British Provincial Geographical Societies," in F. Driver and G. Rose, eds., *Nature and Science: Essays in the History of Geographical Knowledge* (London: Historical Geography Research Group of the Institute of British Geographers, 1992).

13. T. Richards, *The Commodity Culture of Victorian England: Advertising and Spectacle, 1851–1914* (Stanford: Stanford University Press, 1990).

14. Richards 1990, 151.

15. This raises questions about whether Kingsley's gender identity could, parallel with trade, enable her to transcend the boundaries of different areas of imperial control. I discuss this in Chapters 3 and 4.

16. R. West, *Brazza of the Congo—European Exploration and Exploitation in French Equatorial Africa* (London: Jonathan Cape, 1972). Also see Alexander 1991, 7–8. I am using Kingsley's spelling rather than the current spelling for, for example, the Ogooué and Remboué rivers.

17. West 1972. See Chapter 4, this volume, for further discussion of imperial politics and Kingsley's support of trade in West Africa.

18. Mary Kingsley to Dr. Günther, December 11, 1894.

19. M. H. Kingsley, *West African Studies* (London: Macmillan, 1899b). She also published M. H. Kingsley, *The Story of West Africa* (London: Horace Marshall, 1900), and a collection of her father's writings, G. H. Kingsley, *Notes on Sport and Travel* (London: Macmillan, 1900).

20. As noted by both Birkett 1992 and Frank 1986a, Kingsley entered her age as thirty-five on nursing records to keep her near-illegitimacy secret. This incorrect age was engraved on the plaque on her coffin.

21. Kingsley 1899a.

CHAPTER 2

Departure

TRAVEL WRITING AND
GENDERED SUBJECTIVITY

In this chapter I consider departure in the sense of the preparations for travel as well as constructions of subjectivity at home. At this stage, I focus on gendered subjectivity to discuss how this influenced the logistical preparations for departure in terms of conduct books, motives for travel, and the scale and expectations of the journey. Although I emphasize constructions of gender in the context of patriarchy at home and do not look at constructions of, for example, race and class in the context of imperialism while traveling until Chapter 3, these elements were inseparable in the constitution of subjectivity. I hope to illustrate their spatial differentiation, and though I recognize the broad parameters of patriarchy at home and imperialism while traveling, I hope to overcome any false polarity by discussing the construction of gender both prior to and during travel. In this way, I perceive "departure" to include gendered subjectivity while traveling as well as at the point of departure. I discuss the textualization of gender difference in the writings of Kingsley, emphasizing how representations of gender changed over space and time in her self-perception and her perceptions of others, notably African women.[1] Overall, I discuss the relationships between travel writing and ethnographic observation and representation. Initially, however, I outline the epistemological implications of studying the writings by one author—and the study of an individual more generally—in light of poststructuralist claims for the "death of the author." In this context, I consider the significance of the gendering of authorial subjectivity as well as authority.

GENDERED AUTHORSHIP AND AUTHORITY

From a poststructuralist perspective, multiple interpretations of a text should be seen as unconstrained by attempts to discern a single meaning intended by the author because

> as institution, the author is dead: his [*sic*] civil status, his biographical person have disappeared; dispossessed, they no longer exercise over his work the formidable paternity whose account literary history, teaching and public opinion had the responsibility of establishing and renewing.[2]

The "death of the author" seems contrary to the gendering of authorial subjectivity whereby the conditions under which men and women write are materially different, the social construction of gender affects how the writings of men and women are read, and the interpretations of texts are influenced by the gender consciousness of individual readers. Patriarchal discourses locate women both inside and outside culture and, more specifically, both inside and outside constructions of "literature," making the feminine primarily an object rather than subject of the gaze and thus desire.[3] In the case of imperial women travel writers, clear parallels exist between their position as insiders and outsiders in different cultures and their desire to look, which is undermined as they themselves become the object of the look. I discuss the relations between masculinity and subjectivity, femininity and objectivity in terms of complexities and ambivalence in the textual representations of gender difference.

For Michel Foucault, notions of authorship reflect the critical "*individualization* in the history of ideas, knowledge, literature, philosophy, and the sciences"[4] whereby the figure of the author came to be perceived to exist before and beyond rather than in the text. The author's absence from the text was produced by and itself reproduced a position of privileged distance. Paradoxically, notions of "the work" and "writing" have "hindered us from taking full measure of the author's disappearance, blurring and concealing the moment of this effacement and subtly preserving the author's existence."[5] Foucault refers to the "author-function," which reflects the "existence, circulation, and functioning of certain discourses within a society"[6] pertaining to authenticity and authority. According to

Foucault, the author-function split in the eighteenth or nineteenth century, when scientific discourse came to legitimize anonymity in the quest for "truth." In contrast, literary discourse came to stress the importance of the author to an unprecedented degree.[7] In light of this claim, travel writing seems distinctive because of the ways its content often seem to bridge such a divide, as well as the way in which the author as narrator is also the traveler.

For Foucault, authorial presence has been replaced by the author-function, which relates to the conditions for the articulation of discourses rather than their individual, centered authority. In this way, the author as subject comes to represent "a variable and complex function of discourse,"[8] and meaning is not limited to the ideologically significant figure of authorial authority. Ultimately, the author-function would, according to Foucault, prompt the question, "What difference does it make who is speaking?"[9]

It is important to deconstruct perceptions of the stable unity of meaning away from an authoritative authorial presence. However, as long as subjectivity continues to be constructed along lines of difference and power is exercised by defining, legitimating, and exploiting such differences, the ability to fulfill an "author-function" is not universal. Because of this, it seems more useful to refer to *author positionality* in terms of constructions of subjectivity and marginality to dominant, often hegemonic, discursive formations. According to Cheryl Walker,

> what we need, instead of a theory of the death of the author, is a new concept of authorship that does not naively assert that the writer is an originating genius, creating aesthetic objects outside of history, but does not diminish the importance of difference and agency in the responses of [marginalized groups such as] women writers to historical formations.[10]

Walker has also outlined "persona criticism," which reclaims authorship in multiple, intertextual ways and represents "an attempt to connect what is peculiar in a writer's work to what is shared with others."[11] A persona is like a mask rather than a monolithic authorial position. Authorship is composed of complex and sometimes contradictory meanings beyond fixed biography. Because such meanings are multiple within a text, different personae can be interpreted. This contributes to a sense of author positionality, as textual unity is not fixed by the figure of individual authority. The author should be seen as one among multiple presences behind a text and as positioned in multiple ways within a text through different personae. This destabilization of authorial authority suggests that the text only then acquires meanings through the interpretations arising from the reflexivity of reading.

To refer to author positionality, and the study of individuals more generally within the context of poststructuralism, relates to the *sites* at which identities are constructed and contested and therefore illuminates many discursive fields that are inseparable from wider matrices of power and authority. Gendered subjectivity is an important element in the construction of identity, and the conditions under which writing takes place, what is written, and how it is read are inseparable from the gender of the author. Feminist literary theory and criticism have changed over time in ways similar to the study of women in, for example, history and geography, moving from essentialist attempts to make women the subject of inquiry to more profound critiques of subjectivity itself, recognition of constructions of difference, and calls for strategic essentialism. I outline early attempts to describe a female literary tradition to place women travel writers within the general historical context of writing by women.

Elaine Showalter has identified three phases in the development of a Western women's literary tradition in English, beginning with a "feminine" phase of about 1840–1880 involving the imitation of male writing and a focus on the domestic sphere; a "feminist" phase of around 1880–1920 characterized by opposition to masculine values and domination; and, finally, a "female" phase since about 1920 marked by a consciousness of female identity and self-discovery.[12] Although this classification is highly simplistic, it is useful to highlight broad changes over time. It is significant that women's travel writing at the end of the nineteenth century appears to bridge the first two phases, and in Chapter 4 and the Postlude I discuss the extent to which discourses of femininity interacted and conflicted with discourses of feminism.

According to Ellen Moers, the motif of travel has been important in women's literature and, in the "feminine" phase, can be differentiated between indoor and outdoor travel. In the former case, for example, "in the long, dark, twisting, haunted passageways of the Gothic castle, there is travel with danger, travel with exertion—a challenge to the heroine's enterprise, resolution, ingenuity, and physical strength."[13] However, the heroine upheld her respectability of being located indoors.

In contrast, outdoor travel relates to imaginary, romantic themes, with the attraction of travel beyond domestic limits existing largely because of its unattainability. I discuss the ways in which women travel writers such as Kingsley could overcome domestic confinement and definition in terms of their construction when leaving their home sphere, and the gendering of their author positionality as they wrote about their travels.

It is possible to argue that travel writing reflects a duality between narration and description in its ordering, with the former first and most important, and the latter second and subordinate. However, by the late nineteenth century, these two features were often equally important, and travel was often written about in two separate volumes.[14] In the case of Kingsley, *Travels in West Africa* was a largely descriptive narrative about her second journey, appealing to a popular audience, whereas *West African Studies* developed her political proposals and presented her research on, most notably, fetish, which she defined as "the religion of the natives of the Western Coast of Africa, where they have not been influenced either by Christianity or Mohammedanism."[15] These books also differed in the presentation of authorial authority in the introductions to each chapter, which are written in the passive, more distant, voice; in the former, Kingsley was referred to as "the traveler," but in the latter as "the student," consistent with the titles of each book.

Travels in West Africa was published in January 1897, and by June five editions were in circulation, including an abridged version for a wider audience.[16] In the book's first year, the publisher, Macmillan, made £3,000, indicating its wide success.[17] Kingsley's correspondence with Macmillan began in July 1893 concerning the publication of a collection of her father's work. The first mention of a book of her own was made in December 1894, with Kingsley lamenting the disorganization of her "well-intentioned word swamp."[18] Even at this early stage, Macmillan had interpreted her voice as masculine in tone, with Kingsley indignantly responding, "I do not understand what you mean by 'the story being told by a man.' Where have I said it was?"[19]

In the same letter, questions of gendered identity and authorship arose in terms of how she would be named:

> Of course I would rather not publish it under my own name, and I really cannot draw the trail of the petticoat over the Coast of all places—neither can I have a picture of myself in trousers or any other little excitement of that sort added. I went out there as a naturalist not as a sort of circus, but if you would like my name, will it not be sufficient to put M. H. Kingsley?—it does not matter to the general public what I am as long as I tell them the truth as well as I can—I have written it all with my eye on the "Coast" who will of course know I was a lady and will also be the only people who will know the value of what I say, and I do not wish to appear ridiculous or unladylike before them.[20]

Kingsley based *Travels in West Africa* on diaries[21] and letters she wrote to friends. On one level, this reveals different, layered sites of authorship: Kingsley wrote about West Africa while in England but used her own writings from West Africa as source material. On another level, it is clearly problematic to think of travel writing as autobiographical, but this seems increasingly possible when sources like these have been used. The use of information from such private and personal sources is made more explicitly known in travel writing by women than by men,[22] paradoxically reinforcing notions of an individual author yet at the same time, by highlighting personal and potentially more emotional contexts, undermining the authority of that author as a neutral observer.

The influence of individuals besides the author in the production of a text serves to qualify notions of authority. *Travels in West Africa* was edited by Henry Guillemard, who had been appointed as the first lecturer in geography at Cambridge University in 1888.[23] Kingsley, however, denied this level of involvement in her preface; after acknowledging Guillemard's help, she wrote that he

> has not edited it, or of course the whole thing would have been better, but . . . has most kindly gone through the proof sheets, lassoing prepositions which were straying outside their sentence stockade, taking my eye off the water cask and fixing it on the scenery where I wanted it to be, saying firmly in pencil on margins "No you don't," where I committed some more than usually heinous literary crime, and so on. In cases where his activities in these things may seem to the reader to have been wanting, I beg to state that they really were

not. It is I who have declined to ascend to a higher level of lucidity and correctness of diction than I am fitted for.[24]

In this passage, despite her self-effacing tone, Kingsley clearly establishes her individual identity and authority. However, in her letters to Macmillan, her frustration with Guillemard is obvious, suggesting that this public voice of authority was contested in private; for example, in August 1896 she stated that

> I would rather take a 200 ton vessel up a creek than write any book [that incorporates Guillemard's corrections, which] make the thing read easier and more patronising and presuming—"appalling" for simply awful—"dwelling" for house[—] "terminals" for ends—"informed us that" for he said and so on.[25]

Kingsley believed that her appendix on trade and labor was the most important part of the book and was vehement in her assertion that this should be revised by "Liverpool experts" and not by Guillemard, who "knows nothing about it."[26] In this way, Kingsley exercised authority that resulted in her individual authority as an author being both undermined and legitimated.

To view the author as transcendent in her or his authority over and above the text perpetuates the fiction of the unproblematic unity of both text and subject.[27] I discuss the plurality of voices within *Travels in West Africa* in terms of the gendered subjectivity of Kingsley's representations of herself and others to further undermine perceptions of a stable, centered author. Initially, however, I discuss the gendering of subjectivity prior to travel in terms of preparations for departure.

PREPARATIONS FOR DEPARTURE

Motives for Travel

For women such as Kingsley, travel abroad facilitated "a freedom of action unthinkable at home"[28] but often could be realized only when they were freed from domestic responsibilities. Kingsley traveled only after the death of her parents and, even then, only when her brother was abroad and did not demand her services as a housekeeper. Despite—and because of—her evident sense of familial responsibility, Kingsley found it necessary to legitimize her desire to travel. The motives she cited changed as she became better known. For example, in *Travels in West Africa*, there is

> a charming but wholly misleading account, for Mary had become obsessed with West Africa ten and fifteen years earlier while reading Burton, Du Chaillu, and Brazza. . . . Nothing could have been more premeditated, less like the whim she jauntily writes of here.[29]

When she was more prominent, her travels came to appear more planned but in terms of her duty to complete her father's anthropological work. For example, she wrote in 1899 that

> it was the study of early religion and law, and for it, I had to go to West Africa, and I went there, proceeding on the even tenour of my way, doing odd jobs, and trying to understand things, pursuing knowledge under difficulties with unbroken devotion.[30]

However, her father's unfinished book had not yet begun to take shape; rather, it was still a mass of uncodified information, and Kingsley published two of her own books before she turned to a collection of her father's work.[31] Yet Kingsley's use of his writings as a motive for her travels reflects her dual desire to be seen to be fulfilling "feminine duty" at the same time as gaining scientific legitimacy. The motives she cited in *West African Studies* seem more planned, reflecting her desire to legitimize her "studies" more than her "travels." Her tone implies an intellectual duty to travel to West Africa, establishing the authority of her own direct observation:

> For the past fifteen years I have been reading up [*sic*] Africa. . . . I found I had to go down into the most unfashionable part of Africa myself, to try to find out whatever the thing was really like, and also to discover which of my authors had been doing the heaviest amount of lying.[32]

The general climate concerning travel in West Africa was largely discouraging, as shown by the "curious information" Kingsley received before departing, which emphasized "the dangers . . . disagreeables . . . [and] diseases of West Africa."[33] In this list, the position of the traveler seems largely logistical and is reduced to "the things you must take . . . the things you find most handy . . . [and] the worst possible things you can do in West Africa."[34] Before discussing Kingsley's preparations for departure, I outline conduct books to illustrate the gendering of those perceived, and who perceive themselves, as travelers.

Conduct Books

Books for male travelers[35] emphasized methods and equipment necessary for scientific observation and the management of indigenous servants, while books for women travelers often focused on the appropriate behavior of the traveler herself. This distinction reflects the professionalization of male travel in contrast to the personalization of female travel. Francis Galton described travel as a career and listed the necessary qualifications as follows:

> If you have health, a great craving for adventure, at least a moderate fortune, and can set your heart on a definite object, which old travelers do not think impracticable, then—travel by all means. If in addition to these qualifications, you have scientific taste and knowledge, I believe that no career, in time of peace, can offer to you more advantages than that of a traveler.[36]

Travel was seen to offer particular advantages for scientific observation to "a man prepared to profit by them" because

> he sees Nature working by herself, without the interference of human intelligence; and he sees her from new points of view; he has also undisturbed leisure for the problems which perpetually attract his attention by their novelty.[37]

In other accounts, scientific observation was seen as an essential component of imperial duty; for example, the Royal Geographical Society stressed that

> it is the duty of every civilised traveller in countries newly opened up to research, to collect facts, plain unvarnished facts, for the information of those leading minds of the age who, by dint of great experience, can ably generalise from the details contributed from diverse sources.[38]

In this way the individual observations contributed to the collective, imperialist enterprise of pursuing knowledge and, because of the emphasis on "facts," to the understanding of "truth."

The components and weight of the traveler's outfit was a major consideration for both Galton and the RGS. Galton was particularly specific in listing "essential" items, which were disproportionate according to race. Stores "for each white man" would weigh 66 pounds, with an additional 44 pounds of provisions for each six months; these necessities were, however, more than halved "for each black man," who would require stores weighing 30 pounds and six-monthly supplies of 17 pounds.[39] The main difference was the amount of clothes and bedding, with the traveler requiring 30 pounds in contrast to his servants' 9 pounds.[40] One final example illustrates the scale of a recommended outfit, in this case for an African expedition. Although "the absolute necessity for extreme moderation in the use of alcohol" is stressed, the RGS *Hints to Travellers* advised that

> for an expedition not likely to last more than a year, the following amount will be found sufficient: two dozen of good champagne, three bottles of sherry, four bottles of brandy, and four of whiskey.[41]

Another central concern of both accounts was the appropriate management of indigenous servants while traveling. It becomes of paramount importance to maintain both racial and class superiority by adopting a brisk but, in the traveler's opinion, essentially good-humored tone of command. For example, the RGS advised that

> in all dealings with camp-servants and natives be first of all patient, next just and firm, dealing praise and blame alike sparingly, but heartily. Never lose your temper—except on purpose, and avoid banter.[42]

In a similar way, Galton advised the adoption of a "frank, joking, but determined manner, joined with an air of showing more confidence in the good faith of the natives than you really feel,"[43] and he perpetuated the popular distance between a "civilised" traveler/observer and "savage" native by stating,

> If a savage does mischief, look on him as you would on a kicking mule, or a wild animal, whose nature it is to be unruly and vicious, and keep

your temper quite unruffled. Evade the mischief, if you can: if you cannot, endure it; and do not trouble yourself overmuch about your dignity, or about retaliating on the man, except it be on the grounds of expediency.[44]

In contrast to these two books, conduct books written for women travelers concentrated on the appropriate behavior of the traveler largely independently from her interaction with others and in terms of fulfilling behavioral rather than scientific expectations. Conduct books represent one arena for the public discourse of bourgeois society, reflecting the ideological significance of literature.[45] Two transformations in the history of conduct books can be identified: the Enlightenment of the eighteenth century was marked by books constructing the ideal of a domestic woman, replacing courtesy literature that portrayed aristocratic behavior as the ideal to which both men and women should aspire; then emerged, in the nineteenth century, a "beauty system" whereby women came to be represented as objects requiring improvement to aspire to constructed images of femininity.[46] Such historical change rested on the increasingly explicit gendering of conduct, and in this context conduct books imposed discursive rules on the behavior of women in patriarchal society.[47]

The articulation and reproduction of patriarchal discourses through the ideology of conduct can be illustrated by two books written for women travelers in the late nineteenth century. The first, *A Few Words of Advice on Travelling and Its Requirements Addressed to Ladies*, was published in 1875 and was in its fourth edition by 1878.[48] Its publication by Thomas Cook—and the inclusion of, for example, a section on "souvenirs, and where to buy them"; French and German vocabularies; and tables charting distance, weather, and continental weights and measures—suggests that this book was written for early tourists. It reads like a guidebook, but rather than describing a particular place (it included references to places as far from each other as Algeria and Australia[49]), it was addressed primarily to a particular readership, as explained in the opening sentence:

> It is a strange but actual fact that though guide-books and hints to travellers have been written in legion, none have hitherto specially and efficiently devoted a space to the travelling requirements of ladies.[50]

Such feminine "requirements" included tours suitable for different seasons, things most likely to be forgotten, suitable luggage, and what to wear. The feminization of travel in this case involved for the most part an emphasis on appearance and the responsibility for packing necessities from home. Suitable "outfits" were described in detail and assumed national as well as personal importance. The following statement implies that—if only for the sake of appearances—it was a matter of feminine duty to defend national pride and honor:

> Is the credit of our own country nothing to us, that we should be content to rest under the assertion that Englishwomen, though renowned for their beauty, are as a rule the worst dressers in the world? A little care in choosing and in the manner of wearing articles of dress would soon put us on a level with our critics.[51]

In contrast, Lilias Campbell Davidson's *Hints to Lady Travellers at Home and Abroad* of 1889 considered general travel for women rather than specific tours.[52] This alphabetical guide that went from "accidents" to "yachting" included ninety-one entries, ranging from "etiquette" to more starkly material concerns such as "teapots" and "wedges for doors." This text attempted to inform women how to maintain respectability while violating the codes of society by traveling beyond the domestic sphere. As discussed by Mills, several "hints" were oriented to making public spaces private and feminine in their domesticity.[53] Although Davidson referred to the "lady" traveler as "her own escorted and independent person,"[54] travel for women was equated with danger and the inferiority of women was stressed. The entry for "accidents" illustrates the helpless passivity promoted by the ideology of feminine conduct and the tone of deference with which it was textually represented:

> Fortunately, courage and calmness in the hour of peril are no longer rare feminine virtues in the present day, and even where they have not been bestowed by nature, they may very easily be acquired by cultivation and education. As a broad general principle, a woman's place in the moment of danger is to keep still and be ready for action. It is so much an instinct with the stronger sex to protect and look after the weaker, that in all cases of the sort, if there is a man at the head of affairs, he had better be left to manage matters without

the hampering interference of feminine physical weakness. If there is no man, the woman will have to act for herself, but even then she will find it the best plan to keep still till the decisive moment arrives.[55]

Sexual harassment was another potential danger while traveling, but was attributed to female rather than male behavior. According to Davidson, in all cases with which she had been familiar, "the woman has had only herself to blame,"[56] and she proceeded to state that

> I am quite sure that no man, however audacious, will, at all events if he be sober, venture to treat with undue familiarity or rudeness a woman, however young, who distinctly shows him by her dignity of manner and conduct that any such liberty will be an insult. As a rule, women travelling alone receive far more consideration and kindness from men of all classes than under any other circumstances whatever, and the greater independence of women, which permits even young girls, in these days, to travel about entirely alone, unattended even by a maid, has very rarely inconvenient consequences.[57]

The threat of sexual harassment is thus minimized, any potential danger arises from the behavior of the woman rather than the man, and the independence of travel is, ironically, achieved only by acknowledging feminine inferiority and dependence on men.

Further examples that illustrate the construction of feminine codes of conduct while traveling include the claim that a "calm serenity of spirit is really one of the most excellent things for keeping one cool on a melting day,"[58] and discussion of a delicate appetite, the appropriate length and exertion of walks, and feminine frailty:

> The struggle to make a respectable breakfast is not half such a price to pay as a whole day to follow of neuralgia, sick headache, exhaustion, ruffled nerves, and a thousand and one feminine miseries.[59]

Although this conduct book seems to address universal standards of feminine behavior, it was directed at a particular class of women travelers. A fixed social hierarchy was assumed and seemed to override constructions of gender; in this way "lady's maids" were seen as a "great nuisance, as a rule, [because] . . . the majority . . . are weak and impotent things in travelling."[60] In addition, with regard to train carriages reserved for women on long-distance journeys,

> the occupants are seldom of an order to invite one's longings to have them as fellow-passengers, and consist, as a general rule . . . of babies-in-arms with their natural guardians, and of aggressive-looking females, who certainly do not strike the beholder as in any way needing the sheltering shield of a carriage specially dedicated to unprotected females.[61]

These examples illustrate that such codes of feminine conduct were not intended to be universal; rather, they were directed primarily at upper- and middle-class women who perceived themselves as different from both women of lower classes and women who did not conform to their standards of appropriate feminine behavior. Such standards thus became self-perpetuating in their exclusivity.

Kingsley was familiar with the RGS *Hints to Travellers*, but even if she had not read books specifically written for women travelers, it remains important to discuss such conduct books because of the ways they influenced general perceptions of women travelers. Kingsley's references to the former book parody both her own position as a woman traveler and the nature and authority of such books. For example, she suggested that

> the Royal Geographical Society ought to insert among their "Hints" that every traveller in this region should carefully learn every separate native word, or set of words, signifying "I don't know,"—four villages and two rivers I have come across out here solemnly set down with various forms of this statement, for their native name.[62]

During her ascent of Mount Cameroon, Kingsley referred to the standards set by the RGS in parodying herself as an explorer dependent on an African servant:

> Nice situation this: a madman on a mountain in the mist. Xenia, I found, had no longer got my black bag, but in its place a lid of a saucepan and an empty lantern. To put it mildly, this is not the sort of outfit the R.G.S. *Hints to Travellers* would recommend for African exploration.[63]

A final example illustrates how Kingsley adopted a tone of self-mockery to legitimize her single status by referring to the *Hints to*

Travellers. When questioned by an official concerned by her desire to travel through the rapids on the Ogowé River, she replied that

> neither the Royal Geographical Society's list, in their "Hints to Travelers," nor Messrs. Silver, in their elaborate lists of articles necessary for a traveller in tropical climates, make mention of husbands.[64]

The Logistics of Travel

The scale of Kingsley's journeys was considerably smaller than that envisioned and recommended by books such as *Hints to Travellers*. Unlike, for example, Stanley's 300 porters or the 44 canoes and more than 700 men accompanying De Brazza by his third journey, Kingsley's guides never exceeded nine men.[65] The small size of an entourage allowed it to travel and arrive in settlements unheralded and provided the potential for more direct, personal contact between the traveler and people and places encountered.

Grants for travel were disproportionately available according to the gender of the traveler. Male travelers could receive significant financial backing, as when, for example, the *New York Herald* and the *Daily Telegraph* combined to offer Stanley £12,000 for his 1874–1877 trans-African journey.[66] Grants and other forms of material and informational support were available to men through their membership in societies: the RGS offered relatively large sums for male travelers, who nevertheless consistently complained that they were insufficient to cover costs, whereas no woman traveler received money from the RGS in the nineteenth century.[67] Kingsley took £300 on her first journey and traveled as a trader to pay her way.[68] Because of their dependence on private sources of income and resources to travel, most women travelers at this time were at least middle class. On their return, they could publish travel accounts to gain a new source of income, which they often channeled directly into further travels. Financial considerations were a central motivation for the publication of *Travels in West Africa*, with Kingsley writing to Macmillan that

> I am anxious to make money because I am now more than ever sure my Brother won't. I have myself only two hundred and sixty pounds a year and that only for fifteen years more—and I keep surviving in

such a pointed way that there is nothing but the work house before me in my old age.[69]

On her return, Kingsley was a very popular speaker but rarely made more than £20 a lecture[70] and was subject to the lower lecture fees and limited venues for women generally. When Kingsley became well known as a traveler and political figure, she received but refused offers of grants, preferring to finance herself through writing and lecturing.[71]

Constructions of gender clearly influenced perceptions of travelers prior to departure, as shown by books addressed to particularly male or female readerships, and the logistics of travel in terms of scale and financing. Motives and expectations also varied in the differential need for legitimation. Essentially, masculine traditions of travel seemed to reflect public, and increasingly professional, perceptions, while women travelers were located within private, more personal spheres of appropriate behavior. Constructions of a traveler's gender continued to be important, and I now turn to Kingsley's self-perceptions and perceptions of others in *Travels in West Africa* in order to illuminate the spatial and temporal discontinuities of such constructions.

GENDERED SUBJECTIVITY OVER SPACE

Textual Representations of Self

The plurality of voices adopted by Kingsley in *Travels in West Africa* undermines perceptions of her stable and unproblematic identity as an author and traveler.[72] Throughout the text, masculine roles of explorer, trader, and scientific observer coexist with feminine self-consciousness about appearance and behavior. Ambiguities of gendered subjectivity are consistently present, arising from temporary license to behave in ways constructed as masculine while traveling but remaining constrained within the context of acceptable feminine conduct.

Kingsley's humor throughout *Travels in West Africa* destabilizes any fixed authority of the narrator and becomes particularly important at moments when there is the potential for conventionally imperialist and masculine statements. This subversion of imperial control and authority seems parallel with claims for "anti-conquest" literature.[73] However, this subversion is inseparable from constructions of gendered identity (which are largely neglected by Pratt), as it also serves to mock both masculine and feminine stereotypes. For example, in her account of navigating along the Rembwé, she told how

> regardless of danger, I grasped the helm, and sent our gallant craft flying before the breeze down the bosom of the great wild river (that's the proper way to put it, but in the interests of science it may be translated into crawling towards the middle).[74]

A further example is her statement that "I have seen at close quarters specimens of the most important big game of Central Africa, and, with the exception of snakes, I have run away from all of them."[75] In both cases, Kingsley sets up a situation of colonial control that she at once subverts by parody.

Clear tensions exist between wanting to be included in a masculine tradition of exploration and seeking some form of self-definition.[76] Essentially,

> in claiming a place in the gallery of white male travellers, Mary Kingsley was claiming more than a mere "explorer" accolade. She was claiming a [spatial and behavioral] freedom from the gender restrictions of her own society, found in the white male status she could assume in Africa.[77]

Kingsley aligned herself with Burton, Stanley, Du Chaillu, and de Brazza[78] but was identifying with a dated tradition because explorers had, by the 1890s, been largely replaced by imperial administrators and, in the case of West Africa, by traders.

The main qualification for being included in a tradition of exploration was achieving a first of some sort. Kingsley was the first European to cross from the Ogowé to the Rembwé by the route she followed and was also the first to ascend Mount Cameroon by its southeast face. These achievements receive the most detailed coverage in *Travels in West Africa*, even though her river passage, for example, was less than 100 miles and took less than a week, unlike the transcontinental journeys of some male explorers.[79] In the case of her climbing Mount Cameroon, Kingsley identified herself as "the third English*man* to ascend the Peak and the first to have ascended it from the south-east face,"[80] illustrating that such achievements were meaningful in terms of nationality and race rather than gender difference.

Kingsley referred to the relative length of explorations, saying that

> the "arm-chair explorer" may be impressed by the greatness of length of the red line route of an explorer; but the person locally acquainted with the region may know that some of those red lines are very easily made in Africa. . . . In other regions a small red line means four hundred times the work and danger, and requires four thousand times the pluck, perseverance and tact. These regions we may call choice spots.[81]

This seems self-defensive in tone and implies Kingsley's authority as someone who is locally acquainted with Africa. She proceeded to advocate the imperialist agenda of exploration whereby the explorer who "makes his long red line pass through great regions of choice spots" and "attains power over their natives, and retains it, welding the districts into a whole, making the flag of his country respected and feared therein, . . . is a very great man indeed."[82]

Kingsley also identified with traders in West Africa, thereby "adopting a male profession and belonging to a community that rarely encountered, and subsequently paid heed to, British gender divisions."[83] Her respect for traders was a consistent theme in her writings and was underpinned by this self-identification; for example, she referred to "old coasters and sea-captains" as "most excellent people, but supremely human. I am one myself now, so I speak with authority."[84] She valued their paternalism, describing traders as "good-hearted, hospitable English gentlemen, who seem to feel it their duty that no harm they can prevent should happen to anyone."[85] Most of all, Kingsley valued the opportunities offered to traders for close contact with African people. She described such contact in a lecture to the Cheltenham Ladies College, explaining that

> the trading method enables you to sit as an honoured guest at far away inland village fires, it enables you to become the confidential friend of that ever powerful factor in all human societies, the old ladies. It enables you to become an associate of that confraternity of

Trading Stores. From Kingsley, West African Studies *(1899).*

Witch Doctors, things that being surrounded with an expedition of
armed men must prevent your doing.[86]

Finally, Kingsley located herself within the masculine tradition
of scientific observation. Relating to masculine endeavors of exploration, trade, and scientific inquiry enabled Kingsley to travel spatially as well as socially beyond the gender restrictions of colonial
settlements constraining women within the domestic sphere. For
example, Kingsley's most vigorous collecting of fish was around
Calabar, suggesting her desire for, and scientific legitimation of,
solitary excursions away from the colonial society of this administrative center.[87] When she writes about her scientific status,
however, her plurality of voices reveals the amibiguities and self-
consciousness of being a woman within a male sphere of activity.
Most often, Kingsley's humor parodies her position as an individual
observer, as when, for example, she described a gorilla: "The old
male rose to his full height (it struck me at the time this was a matter
of ten feet at least, but for scientific purposes allowance must be
made for a lady's emotions)."[88]

Throughout *Travels in West Africa*, Kingsley portrayed herself
within the masculine traditions of exploration, trade, and science
but consistently undercut this with her self-conscious sense of propriety, constructed as feminine. Her location within such masculine traditions while traveling illustrates the mobilization of constructions of gender difference over space, but the coexistence of
masculine and feminine identities highlights ambivalence rather
than fixed, centered constructions of otherness.

Kingsley's concern with her appearance is the most visible
aspect of her perception of, and constraint within, feminine codes
of conduct. For example, she was tempted to buy a leather hat in
Freetown but resisted, stating "I do not feel I could face Piccadilly
in one; and you have no right to go about in Africa in things you
would be ashamed to be seen in at home."[89] Kingsley's negotiation
of masculine and feminine roles and behavior was paralleled by the
lack of a gendered subject in African languages: "I am a most lady-
like old person and yet get constantly called 'Sir.'"[90] Despite this
tone of indignation, Kingsley referred to herself in masculine terms
that are consistently self-deprecating; for example, she stated, "I
am not a literary man,"[91] "I am not by nature a commercial man

myself,"[92] and, finally, that she was "not a family man."[93] Despite such nominal masculinity, she went on to state adamantly,

> I never even wear a masculine collar and tie, and as for encasing the more earthward extremities of my anatomy in—you know what I mean—well, I would rather perish on a public scaffold.[94]

Other references to appropriate dress, however, subvert the ideals of feminine conduct. Throughout *Travels in West Africa* there are many examples of Kingsley's falling—out of bed, through roofs of huts, down wells, and so on—but the most memorable occurred while she was following an indistinct path to the Rembwé River:

> I made a short cut for it and the next news I was in a heap, on a lot of spikes, some fifteen feet or so below ground level, at the bottom of a bag-shaped game pit. It is at these times that you realise the blessing of a good thick skirt. Had I paid heed to the advice of many people in England . . . and adopted masculine garments, I should have been spiked to the bone, and done for. Whereas, save for a good many bruises, here I was with the fulness of my skirt tucked under me, sitting on nine ebony spikes some twelve inches long, in comparative comfort, howling lustily to be hauled out.[95]

Kingsley's identification with masculine traditions of exploration, trade, and scientific observation highlight the primacy of imperial authority through constructions of *racial* difference, while her femininity more specifically underpinned and shaped her self-conscious *national* identity. In this way Kingsley perceived herself not only in relation to racial difference from Africans but also in relation to national difference from other colonizers, and she perceived her appearance and behavior not only in terms of feminine but also national propriety. For example,

> when in Cameroons I had one dress, and one only, that I regarded as fit to support the dignity of a representative of England, so of course when going to call on the representative of another Power I had to put that dress on, and then go out in open boats to warships or for bush walks in it.[96]

Kingsley was most self-consciously aware of her appearance when meeting individuals from other colonizing nations. This applied to both men and women and can be illustrated by two examples, first, when she declined to meet a French nun because she was

> quite certain I should get misunderstood by the gentle, clean, tidy lady, and she might put me down as an ordinary specimen of English-woman, and so I should bring disgrace on my nation. If I had been able to dress up, ashore I could have gone;[97]

and, second, when she prepared to meet a German officer:

> I am in an awful mess—mud-caked skirts, and blood-stained hands and face. Shall I make an exhibition of myself by going unwashed to that unknown German officer who is in charge of the station? Naturally I wash here, standing in the river and swishing the mud out of my skirts; and then wading across to the other bank, I wring out my skirts, but what is life without a towel?[98]

For Kingsley, the alliance between feminine and national respect-ability was characterized by a sense of personal inadequacy. This, however, she expressed in a humorous tone; for example, at one stage she believed that a French official was

> trying to convince the others that I am an English officer in disguise on the spy; which makes me feel embarrassed, and anything but flat-tered. Wish to goodness I knew French, or how to flirt with that French official so as to dispel the illusion.[99]

In Chapter 3 I consider constructions of race and class over space and time; before that, in the following section, I examine Kingsley's perceptions of other people while traveling, in terms of gendered subjectivity. I begin, however, by outlining the implica-tions of gendered subjectivity for ethnographic observation and representation.

Ethnographic Observation and Representation

Current concern with a "crisis of representation" in ethnography has stimulated greater sensitivity to textuality.[100] This relates to the discursive conditions for both writing and the relations of produc-tion rather than the analysis of fixed texts. In this way the partial-ity of ethnographic "truths" is stressed, and experimental writing is often advocated. According to James Clifford, the writing and reading of ethnography are overdetermined by forces ultimately beyond the control of either an author or an interpretive community. These contingencies—of language, rhetoric, power, and history—must now be openly confronted in the process of writing.[101]

The recognition of such contingencies has postcolonial potential to overcome enforced silencing. However, the history of ethnography is rooted in the context of colonialism, and the different interpretations of this situation reflect on current attempts at textual representation of difference. It seems undisputed that

social anthropology emerged as a distinctive discipline at the beginning of the colonial era, that it became a flourishing academic profession toward its close, or that throughout this period its efforts were devoted to a description and analysis—carried out by Europeans, for a European audience—of non-European societies dominated by European power.[102]

I want to focus on the relationship between ethnography and travel writing. Clifford claims that these are usually generically different,[103] but such a claim may perpetuate notions of ethnographic objectivity and authority. In contrast, writings by travelers (as well as by, for example, missionaries, naturalists, and colonial officials) were crucial in providing the empirical basis for the theoretical arguments of comparative ethnologists.[104] Overall,

the strategy of defining itself by contrast to adjacent and antecedent discourses limits ethnography's ability to explain or examine itself as a kind of writing. To the extent that it legitimates itself by opposition to other kinds of writing, ethnography blinds itself to the fact that its own discursive practices were often inherited from these other genres and are still shared with them today.[105]

For example, personal narratives may seem more akin to travel writing but remain central components of ethnographies, although they are often published as separate volumes or are clearly bounded within texts as introductions or first chapters.[106] This ambiguous status of the personal account is underpinned by the paradox of ethnographic authority and its textualization:

Fieldwork produces a kind of authority that is anchored to a large extent in subjective, sensuous experience. One experiences the indigenous environment and lifeways for oneself, sees with one's own eyes, even plays some roles, albeit contrived ones, in the daily life of the community. But the professional text to result from such an encounter is supposed to conform to the norms of a scientific discourse whose authority resides in the absolute effacement of the speaking and experiencing subject.[107]

Parallel with his attempt to separate travel writing from ethnography, Clifford's neglect of feminist critiques of ethnographic writing perpetuates attempts at representation that are not grounded in the constructed and ambivalent subjectivities of those writing, reading, and being represented in ethnographic accounts.[108] Gendered subjectivity is inseparable from all stages and forms of ethnographic representation. In the next section I discuss Kingsley's textual representations of people she encountered while traveling to illustrate the complexities of gender and its interaction with race in informing perceptions of difference by a Western woman in the context of colonization. This relates to a critique of perceptions of a crisis of representation that are based on the unfounded assumptions that, first, travel writing is generically different from ethnography and that, second, ethnographic authority can be considered without foregrounding constructions of gender difference. By focusing on the writings of Kingsley, I address the claim that women ethnographers in the nineteenth and twentieth centuries

> negotiate femininity in relation to disciplinarity (its authority as a unitary discourse, the constitution of authority as a male preserve), to identity (of authentic/inauthentic criteria, claims for competing identities within the ethnographic monograph) and to cultural difference (femininity written in a different cultural inscription).[109]

Textual Representations of Others

Throughout *Travels in West Africa*, Kingsley was consistently anxious to establish credibility as a scientific observer, emphasizing, for example, that "I have written only on things that I know from personal experience and very careful observation"[110] and stressing "my own extensive experience of the West Coast."[111] In addition, Kingsley stated that "unless you live among the natives, you never get to know them; if you do this you gradually get a light into the true state of their mind-forest."[112] Observation is, however, clearly reflexive, and in the discussion that follows I illustrate ways in which Kingsley attempted to be identified as an objective, masculine observer while maintaining more feminine characteristics of subjective observation. In this way, the authority of observation seems dependent on gendered subjectivity, masculine and feminine voices coexisted to undermine such authority, and Kingsley's accounts of *other* people reveal as much, if not more, about her*self*.

Kingsley perceived gender difference in essentialist terms whereby "men are men and women are women all the world over"[113] and "just as your African man is the normal man, so is your African woman the normal woman."[114] She also believed in the essentialist nature of racial difference, "not of degree but of kind,"[115] and likened this to the difference "between men and women among ourselves. A great woman, either mentally or physically, will excel an indifferent man, but no woman ever equals a really great man."[116] For Kingsley, clear axes of difference existed whereby she saw herself as inferior in terms of gender while at home but racially superior while traveling. Her representations of other people—colonizers and colonized, men and women—thus have implications for whether and how notions of gender difference coexisted with racial difference.

A further generalization parodies her notions of essential masculinity and notions of feminine duty and service:

> Remember that whenever you see a man, black or white, filled with a nameless longing, it is tobacco he requires. Grim despair accompanied by a gusty temper indicates something wrong with his pipe, in which case offer him a straightened-out hairpin.[117]

It is notable that within *Travels in West Africa*, male colonizers are referred to, either by name or as anonymous officials or traders, but personal encounters and characterizations remain largely undeveloped. Kingsley identified most closely with traders, but these men were textualized as a body rather than as individuals. Her personal contact with individual traders seems more pronounced in her political activity on her return home. Such contact was established through her prolific letter writing,[118] suggesting a distinction between her public and private writings. She was conscious of her gender inferiority to male colonizers while traveling and in her

travel writing but, on her return home, transcended such perceptions in the private sphere of correspondence that, ironically, underpinned her public, political identity.

In her contact with African men, Kingsley's relationship with
the Fan people receives closest attention and her closest identification in *Travels in West Africa*. These people were at the time
infamous for cannibalism, and Kingsley used this notoriety to establish herself within the masculine tradition of exploration, com-
paring herself with de Brazza, who "got in touch with the Okanda
and Adooma tribes, people less ferocious and more helpful than
the Fans."[119] Kingsley portrayed this relationship in the form of
masculine camaraderie:

> A certain sort of friendship soon arose between the Fans and me. We
> each recognised that we belonged to that same section of the human
> race with whom it is better to drink than to fight.[120]

The cannibalism of the Fans would be taboo if described by someone primarily identified as feminine. However, Kingsley adopts a
brisk, ironic, and humorous tone, saying that

> the cannibalism of the Fans, although a prevalent habit, is no dan-
> ger, I think, to white people, except as regards the bother it gives
> one in preventing one's black companions from getting eaten.[121]

Kingsley was more likely to relate to and reciprocate with
women as individuals. This was particularly marked in the case of
other colonizing women; for example, Lady MacDonald was a "very
sweet and gracious lady,"[122] and although Mary Slessor was a "very
wonderful lady[,] . . . the sort of man [she] represents is rare."[123]
In other cases she discussed colonizing women—always favorably
and individually—in terms of their appearance and conduct, which
highlighted their femininity:

> Madame Forget is a perfectly lovely French girl, with a pale transpar-
> ent skin and the most perfect great dark eyes, with indescribable
> charm, grace of manner, and vivacity in conversation.[124]

Similarly, throughout *Travels in West Africa*, Kingsley emphasized the appearance of African women, although this was more

Fan people. From Kingsley, Travels in West Africa *(1897).*

likely to be on collective rather than individual terms and in a more conventionally sexualized, objectifying way. For example, Kingsley seemed to establish herself as a distanced, potentially masculine observer[125] by stating that

> the "Fanny Po" ladies are celebrated for their beauty all along the West Coast, and very justly. They are not however, as they themselves think, the most beautiful women in this part of the world. Not at least to my way of thinking. I prefer an Elmina, or an Igalwa, or a M'pongwe, or—but I had better stop and own that my affections have got very scattered among the black ladies on the West Coast, and I no sooner remember one lovely creature whose soft eyes, perfect form and winning, pretty ways have captivated me than I think of another.[126]

Such naming and listing served to depersonalize and objectify the women being described and reflected imperialist strategies of control through categorization. This is also clear in Kingsley's generalizations about older women:

Yoruba women. From Kingsley, West African Studies *(1899).*

The usual statements that the African women age—go off, I believe, is the technical term—very early is, I am sure, wrong in many cases. Look at those Sierra Leone mammies, slightly spherical, I own, but undeniably charming; and the Calabar women, although belonging to a very ugly tribe, are very little the worse for twenty years one way or the other.[127]

In a similar way, Kingsley's often detailed descriptions of clothes objectified African women and established a privileged position for herself as viewing subject. The only other characteristic of individual African women she consistently remarked upon was their ability to speak English, reflecting imperialist imperatives.[128]

The most sustained reference to the lives of African women lay in Kingsley's discussion of polygamy, in which she advocated tolerance of this indigenous institution. Like the cannibalism of the Fans, polygamy would have been taboo if discussed by a voice primarily identified as feminine. However, Kingsley cultivated an amused tone of attempted objectivity, arguing that one reason for polygamy was

> that it is totally impossible for one woman to do the whole work of a house—look after the children, prepare and cook the food, prepare the rubber, carry the same to the markets, fetch the daily supply of water from the stream, cultivate the plantation &c.&c. Perhaps I should say it is impossible for the dilatory African woman, for I once had an Irish charwoman, who drank, who would have done the whole week's work of an African village in an afternoon, and then been quite fresh enough to knock some of the nonsense out of her husband's head with that of the broom, and throw a kettle of boiling water or a paraffin lamp at him, if she suspected him of flirting with other ladies.[129]

Although she recognized a sexual division of labor, she did not draw out the common domestic sphere of women among both colonized and colonizers. The juxtaposition of two worlds in such a caricatured way means that her underlying ideas of racial difference were not transcended by a sensitivity to any common female experience. In addition, this description of domestic work differentiates Kingsley in terms of her own class identity because she was in a position to employ another woman to do domestic work for her; furthermore, the charwoman is of a lower class and is thus not judged for falling short of the bourgeois ideals of feminine conduct.

CONCLUSION

In this chapter, I have attempted to reveal the significance, ambivalence, and differentiation of constructions of gendered subjectivity over space and time. I have concentrated on an individual author to emphasize the positionality that arises from many, often conflicting discourses that come together to establish the conditions and constraints for gendered subjectivity and that is expressed through textual representation. In this way I view poststructuralist perceptions of the "death of the author" to relate to the construction of author positionality. By focusing on the writings of Kingsley, I am not celebrating individuality in the sense of a universal, humanistic essence of subjectivity; rather, I am attempting to illustrate the multiple constructions of subjectivity.

I have broadened the meaning of "departure" from one fixed moment in space and time to include constructions of Kingsley's gendered subjectivity while traveling. This is part of an attempt to destabilize distinctions between "home" and away and to represent the complex constructions of space as well as subjectivity. In the context of "home,"[130] I discussed the form of *Travels in West Africa* to illuminate arguments concerning authorial authority as well as preparations for departure, including motives, conduct books, and general logistics. Kingsley's textual representations of herself and others during her travels relate to broader arguments concerning observation and ethnography. All of these examples illustrate the unstable, ambivalent constructions of gender difference that informed and emerged from Kingsley's travels and writings.

To refer to author positionality is therefore very different from notions of unproblematic, fixed authority. Gendered subjectivity is instead constructed and contested in many different ways over space and time. Its textual representation in the writings of Kingsley reflects this complexity and, in the context of contemporary concern with a "crisis of representation," reveals the need to foreground gender difference and to stress its immanence within the ambivalence of colonial representation.

NOTES

1. At this stage I am focusing on writings by Mary Kingsley, particularly *Travels in West Africa* (London: Macmillan, 1897). I discuss reader

responses to her travels and her books, articles, lectures, and letters in Chapter 4 in the context of her return home and particularly her political identity. Prior to her departure, I review what others were writing; during her journey, I discuss Kingsley's own writings; and on her return, I focus on both her own and others' writings. This apparent asymmetry mirrors the material and metaphorical significance of travel, with Kingsley gaining voice while away and reconstituting "home" on her return. It also reflects the limitations of documentary sources, notably regarding perceptions of Kingsley while traveling. Furthermore, although her books were widely reviewed, it is only possible to speculate about who her actual readers were and who Kingsley perceived her readers to be, particularly in terms of gender. In addition, the archives of her correspondence are largely one-sided, consisting of her letters but few replies.

2. R. Barthes, *The Pleasure of the Text*, trans. R. Miller (New York: Hill and Wang, 1975), 27.

3. M. A. Doane, *The Desire to Desire* (Bloomington: Indiana University Press, 1987).

4. M. Foucault, "What Is an Author?" in J. V. Harari, ed., *Textual Strategies: Perspectives in Poststructuralist Criticism* (Ithaca, NY: Cornell University Press, 1979), 141.

5. Ibid., 144.

6. Ibid., 148. Foucault summarizes the "author-function" in the following way: "(1) the author-function is linked to the juridical and institutional system that encompasses, determines, and articulates the universe of discourses; (2) it does not affect all discourses in the same way at all times and in all types of civilization; (3) it is not defined by the spontaneous attribution of a discourse to its producer, but rather by a series of specific and complex operations; (4) it does not refer purely and simply to a real individual, since it can give rise simultaneously to several selves, to several subjects—positions that can be occupied by different classes of individuals" (p. 153). Foucault goes on to acknowledge that his consideration of authorship has been limited to written texts and should also include "painting, music, and other arts" as well as "transdiscursive" authors who "can be the author of a theory, tradition, or discipline in which other books and authors will in turn find a place."

7. Ibid., 149.

8. Ibid., 158.

9. Ibid., 160.

10. C. Walker, "Feminist Literary Criticism and the Author," *Critical Inquiry* 16, 3 (1990): 551–571; p. 560.

11. C. Walker, "Persona Criticism and the Death of the Author," in *Contesting the Subject: Essays in the Postmodern Theory and Practice of Biography and Biographical Criticism*, ed. W. H. Epstein (West Lafayette, IN: Purdue University Press, 1991), 118.

12. E. Showalter, *A Literature of Their Own: Women Novelists from Brontë to Lessing* (Princeton, NJ: Princeton University Press, 1977).

13. E. Moers, *Literary Women* (London: Women's Press, 1978), 129.

14. M. L. Pratt, "Fieldwork in Common Places," in *Writing Culture: The Poetics and Politics of Ethnography*, ed. J. Clifford and G. E. Marcus (Berkeley: University of California Press, 1986a), 35.

15. M. H. Kingsley, *West African Studies* (London: Macmillan, 1899b), 113.

16. Both of Kingsley's books are very long; including appendices, *Travels in West Africa* is over 700 and *West African Studies* over 600 pages.

17. K. Frank, *A Voyager Out: The Life of Mary Kingsley* (Boston: Houghton Mifflin, 1986a). By January 1898 Kingsley had received a royalty cheque for over £500, as acknowledged in a letter from Kingsley to George Macmillan, January 2, 1898. This alone doubled her annual income from her parents' estate, as stated in a letter to George Macmillan written on December 18, 1894, which is quoted below.

18. Mary Kingsley to George Macmillan, December 18, 1894.

19. Ibid.

20. Ibid.

21. Kingsley found it necessary to justify including extracts from her diary, "being informed on excellent authority that publishing a diary is a form of literary crime. . . . Firstly, I have not done it before, for so far I have given a sketchy *resumé* of many diaries kept by me while visiting the regions I have attempted to describe. Secondly, no one expects literature in a book of travel. Thirdly, there are things to be said in favour of the diary form, particularly when it is kept in a little known and wild region, for the reader gets therein notice of things that, although unimportant in themselves, yet go to make up the conditions of life under which men and things exist" (Kingsley 1897, 100).

22. C. Stevenson, *Victorian Women Travel Writers in Africa* (Boston: Twayne, 1982).

23. D. R. Stoddart, *On Geography and Its History* (Oxford: Basil Blackwell, 1986). Stoddart writes that Guillemard was a naturalist who wrote an account of his travels to, among other places, Japan, New Guinea, and Borneo from 1882 to 1884. He resigned his lectureship after only six months, writing later that this was due to failing health, poor teaching equipment, and the lack of a lecture room.

24. Kingsley 1897, xx.

25. Kingsley to Macmillan, August 20, 1896.

26. Kingsley to Macmillan, September 12, 1896.

27. Foucault 1979.

28. D. Middleton, *Victorian Lady Travellers* (London: Routledge and Kegan Paul, 1965).

29. Frank 1986a, 57.

30. M. H. Kingsley, "In the Days of My Youth," *Mainly About People* (May 20, 1899a): 468–469.

31. G. H. Kingsley, *Notes on Sport and Travel* (London: Macmillan, 1900).

32. Kingsley 1899b, 221.

33. Kingsley 1897, 2.

34. Ibid.

35. Male travelers were clearly gendered subjects but are not the focus of my research. See F. Driver, "Geography's Empire: Histories of Geographical Knowledge," *Environment and Planning D: Society and Space* 10 (1992): 23–40. He writes that "the heroes of the colonial land-scape—the explorer, the hunter, the soldier, the missionary, the administrator, the gentleman—were all gendered in particular ways, providing moral models for a generation of empire builders" (p. 27) and points to the neglect of representations of masculinity, among other aspects of the culture of imperialism, by historians of modern geography.

36. F. Galton, *The Art of Travel; or, Shifts and Contrivances Available in Wild Countries*, 7th ed. (London: John Murray, 1883), 1. See D. Middleton, "Francis Galton: Victorian Genius," *Geographical Journal* 141, 2 (1975): 266–269. She writes that Galton's book was a result of his travels in southwest Africa from 1850 to 1852. He received the Founder's Gold Medal of the Royal Geographical Society in 1854, served as honorary secretary from 1857 to 1863, and was almost continuously on the council from 1854 until 1893.

37. Galton 1883, 2.

38. D. W. Freshfield and W. J. L. Wharton, *Hints to Travellers Scientific and General*, 7th ed. (London: Royal Geographical Society, 1893), 446.

39. Galton 1883, 11.

40. Ibid.

41. Freshfield and Wharton 1893, 27.

42. Ibid., 5.

43. Galton 1883, 308.

44. Ibid.

45. See, for example, E. Balibar and P. Macherey, "On Literature as an Ideological Form," in *Untying the Text: A Post-structuralist Reader*, ed. R. Young (Boston: Routledge and Kegan Paul, 1981); L. Davis, *Resisting Novels: Ideology and Fiction* (New York: Methuen, 1987); and H. Roberts, "Propaganda and Ideology in Women's Fiction," in *The Sociology of Literature*, ed. D. Laurenson, Sociological Review Monograph 26 (Keele, England: University of Keele, 1978).

46. *The Ideology of Conduct: Essays in Literature and the History of Sexuality*, ed. N. Armstrong and L. Tennenhouse (New York: Methuen, 1987).

47. M. L. Poovey, *The Proper Lady and the Woman Writer: Ideology as Style in the Works of Mary Wollstonecraft, Mary Shelley, and Jane Austen* (Chicago: University of Chicago Press, 1984).

48. H.M.L.S., *A Few Words of Advice on Travelling and Its Requirements Addressed to Ladies*, 4th ed. (London: Thomas Cook, 1878).

49. References to particular places were wide-ranging and diverse, even including a "Tour around the World." However, the book focused on continental European travel, which was particularly popular for its art

and health resorts and where "travelling has become a comparatively in-expensive luxury" (Ibid., 9).

50. Ibid., vii.

51. Ibid., 12. On the previous page it was suggested that "in choosing each item of the travelling costume, care should be taken to avoid everything *outré* or *conspicuous*. It will be a proud day for Englishwomen when, instead of the remark 'So English' being applied by foreigners to the most awkward and unsuitably-dressed lady they may meet, it will be to the best and most appropriately attired. At present, I am sorry to say, the former mortifying remark may be continually heard."

52. L. C. Davidson, *Hints to Lady Travellers at Home and Abroad* (London: Iliffe, 1889). Despite its title, most of the book addresses travel within the British Isles, although the implications of its codes of conduct would presumably be exacerbated for travel abroad. I will discuss this book at greater length because of its focus on travel generally rather than tourism more specifically.

53. S. Mills, *Discourses of Difference: An Analysis of Women's Travel Writing and Colonialism* (London: Routledge, 1991): 99–103.

54. Davidson 1889, 255.

55. Ibid., 12.

56. Ibid., 63.

57. Ibid.

58. Ibid., 189.

59. Ibid., 70. In addition, in contrast to the amount of alcohol perceived as essential for a man' s traveling outfit, the only beverage referred to by Lilias Campbell Davidson was tea. This, however, seems to possess addictive and intoxicating potential. She claims, for example, that "there can be no doubt that the intemperate use of this most delightful and refreshing beverage is becoming a grave evil amongst Englishwomen" (p. 197) and that "it is a thousand pities to abuse by excess one of the most rational, pleasant, and innocent indulgences which are open to the use of womankind" (p. 198).

60. Ibid., 134.

61. Ibid., 135.

62. Kingsley 1897, 237.

63. Ibid., 578.

64. Ibid., 167.

65. D. Birkett, "An Independent Woman in West Africa: The Case of Mary Kingsley" (Ph.D. thesis, University of London, 1987).

66. Ibid.

67. Ibid. See the Postlude for discussion of the debates concerning the admission of women to the Royal Geographical Society.

68. Frank 1986a.

69. Kingsley to Macmillan, December 18, 1894.

70. Birkett 1987.

71. As shown by an undated letter from Kingsley to George

Macmillan, in which she wrote "nothing will ever persuade me to take a grant—though I have had offers of three good ones, but I am determined to have my finances under my own hand and have 20/- for every 15/- I owe."

72. As discussed by Birkett 1987 and Mills 1991.

73. M. L. Pratt, *Imperial Eyes: Travel Writing and Transculturation* (London: Routledge, 1992).

74. Kingsley 1897, 343.

75. Ibid., 268

76. Birkett 1987.

77. Ibid., 121.

78. For further discussion of African exploration by men, see C. Hibbert, *Africa Explored: Europeans in the Dark Continent, 1769–1889* (Harmondsworth: Penguin, 1982); and T. Pakenham, *The Scramble for Africa, 1876–1912* (London: Wiedenfeld and Nicolson, 1991) .

79. Birkett 1987.

80. Kingsley 1897, 550. My emphasis.

81. Ibid., 353.

82. Ibid.

83. Birkett 1987, 103.

84. Kingsley 1897, 514.

85. Kingsley 1899b, 13.

86. M. H. Kingsley, "A Lecture on West Africa," *Cheltenham Ladies College Magazine*, 38 (Autumn 1898): 264–280; p. 267. Earlier in the same lecture, Kingsley said: "Just put yourself in their place and imagine a gentleman of inky complexion, mainly dressed in red and white paint, human teeth, and leopard tails and not too much of them, suddenly arriving in a village hereabouts. After the first thrill of excitement his appearance gave had passed away, and he was found anxious to sell something, anything, say bootlaces, he would be taken much more calmly than if he showed no desire to do business at all."

87. Birkett 1987.

88. Kingsley 1897, 268.

89. Ibid., 19.

90. Ibid., 502.

91. Kingsley 1899b, xii.

92. Ibid., 6.

93. Ibid., 29.

94. Kingsley 1897, 502.

95. Ibid., 269.

96. Ibid., 622.

97. Ibid., 351.

98. Ibid., 563. Despite this decision, Kingsley goes on to say that "I receive a most kindly welcome from a fair, grey-eyed German gentleman, only unfortunately I see my efforts to appear before him clean and tidy have been quite unavailing, for he views my appearance with unmixed horror, and suggests an instant hot bath. I decline. Men can be trying! How

in the world is anyone going to take a bath in a house with no doors, and only very sketchy wooden window-shutters?"

99. Ibid., 140. A further example of the interaction of feminine and national self-consciousness is Kingsley's statement that "I . . . salve my pride as an Englishwoman with the knowledge that were a Frenchwoman to travel in any of our West Coast settlements, she would have as warm and helpful a welcome as I get here, and I will be femininely spiteful, and say that she would do more harm in the English settlements than ever I did in the French. Think of Mme Jacot, Mme Forget, or Mme Gacon going into Calabar, for example, why there wouldn't be a whole heart left in the place in twenty-four hours!" (Ibid., 157).

100. See, for example, Clifford and Marcus 1986 and J. Clifford, *The Predicament of Culture: Twentieth Century Ethnography, Literature and Art* (Cambridge, MA: Harvard University Press, 1988).

101. J. Clifford, "Introduction: Partial Truths," in Clifford and Marcus 1986, 25.

102. T. Asad, "Anthropology and the Colonial Encounter," in *The Politics of Anthropology: From Colonialism and Sexism toward a View from Below*, ed. G. Huizer and B. Mannheim (The Hague: Mouton, 1979), 90.

103. Clifford and Marcus 1986.

104. G. W. Stocking, *Victorian Anthropology* (New York: Free Press, 1987).

105. M. L. Pratt 1986a, 27.

106. Ibid.

107. Ibid., 32.

108. See, for example, J. Marcus, "Predicated on Gender," *Social Analysis* 29 (December 1990): 136–144, who states that the absence of women from Clifford 1988 means that "what is offered as a critical anthropology or a critique of culture is in fact a critique of masculinist anthropology from a masculinist point of view. This form of the production of critique leaves the discipline largely intact and its relations of power once again obscured" (p. 139).

109. L. Turner, "Feminism, Femininity and Ethnographic Authority," *Women: A Cultural Review* 2, 3 (1991): 238–254; p. 251.

110. Kingsley 1897, xx.

111. Ibid., 62.

112. Ibid., 103. Direct observation was perceived as necessary by Kingsley for personal and scientific legitimation and verification. She advises other travelers of this: "Remember, you must always have your original material—carefully noted down at the time of occurrence—with you, so that you may say in answer to his Why? Because of this, and this, and this" (p. 439).

113. Ibid., 207.

114. Kingsley 1899b, 375.

115. Kingsley 1897, 659. In Chapter 3 I focus on Kingsley's perceptions of racial difference.

116. Ibid., 659.

117. Ibid., 125.

118. This is best illustrated by Kingsley's extensive correspondence with John Holt of Liverpool from November 1897 to March 1900.

119. Kingsley 1897, 355.

120. Ibid., 264.

121. Ibid., 330.

122. Ibid., 12.

123. Ibid., 74. Mary Slessor was a Scottish Presbyterian missionary who lived near Calabar for more than twenty years. For further discussion, see C. McEwan, "Encounters with West African Women: Authority and Constraints in the texts of Victorian Women Travel Writers," in *Sexual/ Textual Colonizations: Women's Colonial and Post-colonial Geographies* (New York: Guilford Press, forthcoming).

124. Kingsley 1897, 152.

125. I am referring to Kingsley's descriptions of indigenous women as potentially masculine rather than, for example, lesbian or bisexual, because Kingsley's articulations of gender difference are more evident than issues of sexual orientation.

126. Kingsley 1897, 72.

127. Ibid., 224.

128. See, for example, ibid., 116, 420, and 423.

129. Ibid., 211. This statement is virtually reproduced in the "Appendix on Trade and Labour in West Africa," also in Kingsley, 1897, although here the cross-cultural comparison seems more universalized: "It is perfectly impossible for one African woman to do the work of the house, prepare the food, fetch water, cultivate the plantations, and look after the children attributive to one man. She might do it if she had the work in her of an English or Irish charwoman, but she has not, and a whole villageful of African women do not do the work in a week that one of these will do in a day" (p. 662).

130. As discussed at greater length in Chapter 4, this volume.

CHAPTER 3

Journey

SPACE, PLACE,
AND IMPERIAL SUBJECTIVITY

Building on my discussion of gendered subjectivity as a crucial component of temporal and spatial departure, I now focus on imperial subjectivity in terms of constructions of racial difference over space. Imperial control relates to the exercise of power and authority over both people and places, and I discuss how constructions of race and gender gave rise to distinctive representations by a woman travel writer, and how such representations were spatially differentiated in their significance and implications. I want to address the ambiguities of, on the one hand, a woman's being constructed as subordinate in terms of gender in the context of patriarchal society but, on the other, her being able to share in the authority of colonizers defined in terms of race in the context of imperialism while she traveled.[1] This relates to notions of a journey in terms of how material and metaphorical movement over space and time influenced Mary Kingsley's opinions on imperial politics and policy as she mediated the spheres of "home" and away. I focus on *West African Studies* because of its political orientation, epitomized by a chapter outlining Kingsley's "Alternative Plan" for the government of British West Africa. However, I begin with a topographical metaphor from *Travels in West Africa* that expresses her views on "civilization." This has important implications for her perceptions of colonized places and people as well as her own position in terms of gender, race, and class identity in textually representing such perceptions:

94

I do not believe that the white race will ever drag the black up their own particular summit in the mountain range of civilisation. Both polygamy and slavery are . . . essential to the well-being of Africa—at any rate for those vast regions of it which are agricultural, and these two institutions will necessitate the African having a summit to himself. Only—alas! for the energetic reformer—the African is not keen on mountaineering in the civilisation range. He prefers remaining down below and being comfortable. He is not conceited about this; he admires the higher culture very much, and the people who inconvenience themselves by going in for it—but do it himself? No. And if he is dragged up into the higher regions of a self-abnegatory religion, six times in ten he falls back damaged, a morally maimed man, into his old swampy country fashion valley.[2]

COLONIZED PLACES

Reading and Writing Landscapes

Kingsley's personal, aesthetic enthusiasm was paramount in her descriptions of colonized landscapes. The subjectivity of her response paradoxically undermines her claims for authority as objective observer, while establishing her as capable of vivid description and more sensual sensitivity. She claims subjective authority by stressing the individuality of her response:

To my taste there is nothing so fascinating as spending a night out in an African forest, or plantation; but I beg you to note I do not advise any one to follow the practice. Nor indeed do I recommend African forest life to any one. Unless you are interested in it and fall under its charm, it is the most awful life in death imaginable. It is like being shut up in a library whose books you cannot read, all the while tormented, terrified, and bored. And if you do fall under its spell, it takes all the colour out of other kinds of living.[3]

The landscape seems to possess magical qualities, accessible only to certain, "interested" individuals, and seems to exercise power over those individuals rather than to submit to their control. It is interesting that Kingsley employs a metaphor of herself as able to read the landscape while others seem illiterate. This reflects, but significantly differs from, current notions of reading landscapes as texts, most notably those developed by James Duncan.

In his interpretation of the royal capital of Kandy in Sri Lanka in the early nineteenth century, Duncan proposes a methodology for the interpretation of landscapes, illuminates the political configuration of landscapes, and analyzes this in the context of a highly specific empirical example.[4] Duncan refers to literal, tangible texts rather than expanding on the metaphorical notion of landscape as text so that the textuality of landscape on a conceptual level is superseded by the intertextuality of a specific example. In this way, the empirical specificities of texts in the Kandyan kingdom are illuminated, but the broader conceptual implications of reading a landscape as text are downplayed. In contrast, Kingsley's reference to the textuality of landscape is more self-conscious in its referentiality, as she locates herself within that landscape.[5] In this chapter, I consider how her position as viewing subject was constructed along lines of gender, racial, and class difference to illustrate the distinctive perceptions of a white, middle-class woman traveling within and between patriarchal and imperial spheres.

To highlight the textuality of landscape has the potential for exploring the discursive constraints for interpreting places and spaces. Duncan does not fulfill this potential because he focuses on a highly specific example from a position of privileged distance. In contrast, to consider the subject positionality of Kingsley emphasizes the construction of multiple identities over space and time and the tensions of being an observer both inside and outside the landscape being represented.

Kingsley located herself both emotionally and spatially in West Africa throughout her travel writing, expressing, for example, that "I am more comfortable there than in England."[6] Within West Africa, Kingsley felt more comfortable traveling through the bush rather than fixed in settlements. With the exception of Glass, she stated that "I dislike West Coast towns as a general rule,"[7] corresponding to her desire to move beyond colonial settlements to fish, explore, and trade. Her vivid descriptions of landscapes while traveling are characterized by their personalization, whereby she becomes part of the landscape in her aesthetic response to it. For example, her description of the rapids on the Ogowé River seems metaphysical in its celebration of the ethereal power of the natural world:

In the darkness round me flitted thousands of fireflies and out beyond this pool of utter night flew by unceasingly the white foam of the rapids; sound there was none save their thunder. The majesty and beauty of the scene fascinated me, and I stood leaning with my back against a rock pinnacle watching it. Do not imagine it gave rise, in what I am pleased to call my mind, to those complicated, poetical reflections natural beauty seems to bring out in other people's minds. It never works that way with me; I just lose all sense of human individuality, all memory of human life, with its grief and worry and doubt, and become part of the atmosphere. If I have a heaven, that will be mine.[8]

Such personalized identification with the landscape seems contrary to the imperial strategies epitomized by the "monarch-of-all-I-survey" genre of travel writing.[9] The former reveals the subjectivity of an observer located within the landscape, while the latter relates to a panoramic gaze objectifying the landscape through the imperial power and authority of an external observer. The latter privileges vision, while the former includes other sensual responses, as shown by Kingsley's references to sound: "Woe! to the man in Africa who cannot stand perpetual uproar. Few things surprised me more than the rarity of silence and the intensity of it when you did get it,"[10] with such "uproar" including

the grunting sigh of relief of the hippos, the strange groaning, whining bark of the crocodiles, the thin cry of the bats, the cough of the leopards, and that unearthly yell that sometimes comes out of the forest in the depths of dark nights.[11]

Rather than establish the landscape as a stage for the exercise of the imperial viewer's power, Kingsley's descriptions of West Africa were more likely to prompt self-questioning, further highlighting her personal and reflexive sensitivity to landscape:

As I sat on the verandah overlooking Victoria and the sea, in the dim soft light of the stars, with the fire-flies round me, and the lights of Victoria away below, and heard the soft rush of the Lukola River, and the sound of the sea-surf on the rocks, and the tom-tomming and singing of the natives, all matching and mingling together, "Why did I come to Africa?" thought I. Why! who would not come to its twin brother hell itself for all the beauty and charm of it.[12]

Landscape Description as Anti-Conquest

For Mary Louise Pratt, the "monarch-of-all-I-survey" genre epitomizes the gendering of travel writing in which men were constructed as explorers by mobilizing the masculine heroic discourse
of discovery.[13] Kingsley's *Travels in West Africa* is cited as the main
exception, in which

> through irony and inversion, she builds her own meaning-making
> apparatus out of the raw materials of the monarchic male discourse
> of domination and intervention. The result . . . is a monarchic female
> voice that asserts its own kind of mastery even as it denies domina-
> tion and parodies power.[14]

Pratt describes this difference in spatial terms by contrasting
"her" "vast and unexplored mangrove swamps . . . with the gleam-
ing promontories her fellow Victorians sought out."[15] The position
of the traveler within these spatial parameters also differed according to gender, with Kingsley implicated within rather than distanced
from the landscape. Pratt portrays Kingsley as an eccentric, intrepid
explorer and perpetuates stereotypical images of women travelers
when she tells of her

> discovering her swamps not by looking down at them or even walk-
> ing around them, but by sloshing zestfully through them in a boat or
> up to her neck in water and slime, swathed in thick skirts and wear-
> ing her boots continuously for weeks on end.[16]

Pratt argues that Kingsley's descriptions are feminized in their
domesticity.[17] She illustrates this by calling the boat Kingsley steers
down the Rembwé at night "a combination [of] bedroom and
kitchen" and by characterizing Kingsley as "the domestic goddess
keeping watch and savoring the solitude of her night vigil."[18]
Kingsley visualizes the landscape, describing

> the great, black, winding river with a pathway in its midst of frosted
> silver where the moonlight struck it; on each side the ink-black man-
> grove walls, and above them the band of stars and moonlit heavens
> that the walls of mangrove allowed one to see,[19]

but such magnificence is only imagined under cover of darkness
because "by daylight the Rembwé scenery was certainly not so

St. Paul do Loanda. From Kingsley, West African Studies (*1899*).

lovely, and might be slept through without a pang."[20] Kingsley's
solitude and her idealization of the landscape contribute to a value
system that rejects the textual strategies of male explorers, which
took the form of "fantasies of dominance and possession, painting
that is simultaneously a material inventory."[21]

The ambivalence of Kingsley's position within imperial discourses of power and authority is clear, but this should also be
extended to her gendered subjectivity. Pratt assumes feminization
and reinforces notions of Kingsley as an eccentric individual rather
than addressing the discursive complexities and ambiguities of
gendered subjectivity. For example, Kingsley clearly relishes her
solitude, but this violates codes of appropriate feminine conduct,
and her responsibility in steering the boat seems contrary to more
conventional notions of feminine passivity.

Pratt locates Kingsley as part of but separate from imperial
goals. This position is seen as textually articulated by her "master-
ful comic irreverence" because

at the same time as it mocks the self-importance and possessiveness of her male counterparts, Kingsley's irony constitutes her own form of mastery, deployed in a swampy world of her own that the explorer-men have not seen or do not want.[22]

Pratt's account is persuasive in its construction of Kingsley's "swampy world," but it reduces the complex ambivalence of her identity constructed in terms of racial and gender difference. Such claims could be extended to the topographic metaphor I cited at the beginning of this chapter, so that confining Kingsley to swamps aligns her gender difference with her own perceptions of the racial difference of Africans. This corresponds to Kingsley's claims for essential differences in terms of race and gender and illustrates her ambivalence as an individual discursively constructed by patriarchal and imperial forms of power and authority. However, another reference to swamps seems to undermine this inferior position, Kingsley stating that "the English love, above all things, settling in, or as near as possible to, a good, reeking, stinking swamp."[23] This spatial subversion of imperial power seems inconsistent with both Kingsley's claims for the peaks of "civilization" as well as Pratt's claims for Kingsley's autonomy confined to the swampy underworld. It also suggests a contrast between the ideals and day-to-day practice of imperial rule, the ambivalence of individuals within such discourses and strategies of control, and the need to avoid making exaggerated claims from isolated passages of text that are informed by perceptions of the individualization of subjectivity.

The appropriateness of locating Kingsley primarily in literal and metaphorical swamps can be questioned by, for example, referring to her ascent of Mount Cameroon, which implicates her both within and outside masculine and imperial discourses. However, Kingsley remains ambivalent, stating "verily I am no mountaineer."[24] She locates herself outside the masculine endeavor of mountaineering but admires and likens its dangers to those of her own travels:

> My most favourite form of literature . . . is accounts of mountaineer-ing exploits. . . . I do not care a row of pins how badly they may be written, and what form of bumble-puppy grammar and composition is employed, as long as the writer will walk along the edge of a preci-pice with a sheer fall of thousands of feet on one side and a sheer wall on the other; or better still crawl up an *arête* with a precipice

on either. Nothing on earth would persuade me to do either of these things myself, but they remind me of bits of country I have been through where you walk a narrow line of security with gulfs of murder looming on each side, and where in exactly the same way you are as safe as if you were in your easy chair at home, as long as you get sufficient holding ground: not on rock in the bush village inhabited by murderous cannibals, but on ideas in those men's and women's minds; and these ideas . . . give you safety.[25]

Just as mountaineering skills can overcome the dangers of the natural world, so Kingsley's intellectual skills can overcome the dangers of the human world. Both are presented as textually gripping for an audience at home.

Although perceiving herself as different from mountaineers, Kingsley did climb Mount Cameroon on her second journey in West Africa. However, her ambivalent polyphony in describing this ascent reveals the ambiguities of being constructed as both inside and outside, and moving between, patriarchal and imperial discourses.

From her earliest sightings of Mount Cameroon, Kingsley both identified with and distanced herself from a masculine tradition of exploration:

Now it is none of my business to go up mountains. There's next to no fish on them in West Africa, and precious little good rank fetish, as the population on them is sparse—the African, like myself, abhorring cool air. Nevertheless, I feel quite sure that no white man has ever looked on the great Peak of Cameroon without a desire arising in his mind to ascend it.[26]

If the panoramic vision achieved through mountaineering epitomizes the "monarch-of-all-I-survey" genre of travel writing, Kingsley's contradictory position in terms of gendered subjectivity also relates to her ambivalence in the context of imperialism. Even though she perceives such temptation as universal for colonizing men, Kingsley stresses her individuality and authority by an ironic characterization of her weakness in succumbing to it:

Do not . . . imagine that the ascent is a common incident in a coaster's life; far from it. The coaster as a rule resists the temptation of Mungo [Mah Lobeh, or Mount Cameroon] firmly, being stronger than I am; moreover, he is busy and only too often fever-stricken in the bargain. But I am the exception, I own.[27]

Kingsley's account of her ascent of Mount Cameroon lacks the lively enthusiasm and good humor of the rest of *Travels in West Africa*. Her gendered subjectivity and her position in the context of imperial power and authority seem particularly ambiguous. For example, her ability to identify with the masculine, imperial trope of panoramic vision is undermined as her view is obscured by mist. Furthermore, on her ascent this obscured vision seems to enhance the natural beauty of the scene, which she perceives in primarily aesthetic rather than strategic terms:

> The white, gauze-like mist comes down from the upper mountain towards us: creeping, twining round, and streaming through the moss-covered tree columns. . . . Soon . . . all the mist streams coalesce and make the atmosphere all their own, wrapping us round in a clammy, chill embrace; it is not that wool-blanket, smothering affair that we were wrapped in down by Buana, but exquisitely delicate. The difference it makes to the beauty of the forest is just the same difference you would get if you put a delicate veil over a pretty woman's face or a sack over her head. In fact, the mist here was exceedingly becoming to the forest's beauty.[28]

The landscape is feminized, but its attraction lies in being veiled rather than being unveiled.

The ambiguity of Kingsley's position as an imperial, gendered subject also emerges in her relations with the Africans in her party on the ascent of Mount Cameroon. She is unable to establish either masculine control or more feminine reciprocity, and the resulting tension contrasts with her camaraderie with the Fans.[29] For example, they set out with insufficient water, she states that "the men are sulky,"[30] and she loses her temper when at one stage the men desert the expedition: "I am obliged to be guarded in my language, because my feelings now are only down to one degree below boiling point."[31] Her relations with her party are by now a source of strain rather than of amusement. The ascent is uncomfortable; Kingsley laments her badly sunburnt face, and they travel through a tornado and a hurricane, suffering "bitter wind and swishing rain."[32] She is undecided about continuing to the peak, lacking both the determination and enthusiasm of previous expeditions. She does continue, but her view is fully obscured by mist. Kingsley described the mist as enhancing the beauty of her ascent, but, from the peak, her inability to see seems to possess symbolic and/or strategic more than aesthetic significance: "There is in me no exultation, but only a deep disgust because the weather has robbed me of my main object in coming here, namely to get a good view."[33]

Kingsley's ascent of Mount Cameroon ironically and ambivalently locates her both inside and outside a masculine, imperialist tradition of exploration, conquest and surveillance, illustrating the complexities and contradictions of subject positionality. Although she is successful in her ascent, she is denied a view, and she describes the expedition as hard work rather than a source of pleasure in itself. This final expedition most closely relates to the masculine tradition of goal-oriented travel accounts rather than more feminine odysseys. Kingsley's lack of success in achieving her goal of a view and the strain of the ascent itself reflect her tenuous position as a woman traveling in the context of masculine, imperial discourses.[34]

COLONIZED PEOPLE

Reading and Writing Racial Difference

Despite identifying personally with her African servants, referring to them by name and often characterizing them as individuals, Kingsley supported her belief in essential racial difference by generalizing about "the African character." By the 1890s, however, such polygenesist ideas were dated and discredited not only because of missionary thought, which emphasized common humanity, but also because of Darwinist thought, which explained difference in terms of evolution.[35]

Traveling changed Kingsley's preconceptions of Africans; as she wrote,

> I confess I like the African on the whole, a thing I never expected to do when I went to the Coast with the idea that he was a degraded, savage, cruel brute; but that is a trifling error you soon get rid of when you know him.[36]

Kingsley's generalizations about race related wholly to male objects of study; for example, she outlined her belief that the true Negro is . . . by far the better man than the Asiatic; he is physically superior, and he is more like an Englishman than the Asiatic; he is a logical, practical man, with feelings that are a credit to him, and are particularly strong in the direction of property. . . . His make of mind is exceedingly like the make of mind of thousands of Englishmen of the stand-no-nonsense, Englishman's-house-is-his-castle type. Yet, withal, a law-abiding man, loving a live lord, holding loudly that women should be kept in their place, yet often grievously henpecked by his wives, and little better than a slave to his mother, whom he loves with a love he gives to none other. This love of his mother is so dominant a factor in his life that it must be taken into consideration in attempting to understand the true Negro.[37]

She perceived African men primarily in terms of race but perceived African women in terms of gender, suggesting that she was able to identify with the masculine, imperial discourses objectifying both racial and gender differences.

Kingsley equated race with nationality in the case of English identity, reflecting hegemonic discourses of imperial control. She outlined her simplistic classification of perceived racial difference only after a disclaimer that paradoxically undercuts and yet establishes the authority of her "feelings":

I openly and honestly own I sincerely detest touching on this race question. For one thing, Science has not finished with it; for another, it belongs to a group of subjects of enormous magnitude, upon which I have no opinion, but merely feelings, and those of a nature which I am informed by superior people would barely be a credit to a cave man of the paleolithic period. My feelings classify the world's inhabitants into Englishmen, by which I mean Teutons at large, Foreigners, and Blacks. Blacks I subdivide into two classes, English Blacks and Foreign Blacks. English Blacks are Africans. Foreign Blacks are Indians, Chinese, and the rest.[38]

Kingsley's teleological view of essential racial difference was both informed by and yet potentially challenged by her perceptions of institutions: although she saw that institutions differed, she considered the need for them as the same; for example, although "the African"

culture does not contain our institutions, lunatic asylums, prisons, workhouses, hospitals &c, he has to deal with the same classes of people who require these things. So with him he deals by means of equivalent institutions, slavery, the lash, and death. . . . It's deplorably low of him, I own, but by what alternative plan of government his can be replaced I do not quite see, under existing conditions.[39]

Gender Difference and Imperial Authority

The ambivalence of women travelers such as Kingsley, who participated in masculine discourses of exploration and imperial power and discerned racial identity by objectifying men, suggests that during travel racial superiority came to supersede gender inferiority. However, such ambivalence was more complex than this distinction implies because of the tensions and contradictions of gaining temporary license to behave in ways constructed as masculine while still aiming to satisfy feminine codes of conduct.

The imperial power and authority arising from constructions of racial difference ran parallel with the legitimation of study and observation primarily defined as a masculine quest for knowledge; in this way, while traveling,

> white women could act without Victorian social conventions, assume (male) professional status, and assert power over Black women and men. Mary Kingsley grasped all these opportunities, assuming the guise of a white male professional to allow her a freedom utterly inconceivable within her own society.[40]

Kingsley's inability to position herself fully and be positioned within such masculine discourses meant that she could, ironically, gain greater influence:

> While the tensions of her adoption of white male status often curtailed her freedom of action, the temporary nature of her different professional disguises gave Kingsley a breadth of knowledge and expertise more rigidly identified Africanists of the period lacked. Not fitting easily into available professional categorizations, she could also swiftly adapt her assumed roles as the audience and circumstances demanded.[41]

Such discursive complexity in the construction of subjectivity varied over space within and between patriarchal and imperial spheres, enabling and constraining the positioning of Kingsley primarily in terms of gender and racial identity as she negotiated such spheres.

Sara Mills has argued that such negotiation was characterized by discursive multiplicity and instability whereby the travels and writings of women both transgressed and conformed to patriarchal and imperial discourses. In this way,

> women travellers could not wholeheartedly speak with the voice of colonial discourse, at least not consistently, firstly because of their role in western society and the way this was structured by discourses of femininity, secondly, because some of them had rejected this role by travelling unchaperoned, and thirdly, because they had few discursive places within western colonial institutions.[42]

The implications of ambivalence can be identified in how women travel writers, themselves constructed as different in terms of gender, identified others in terms of race, and how these perceptions were translated and codified in their attitudes toward imperialism.

Both Dea Birkett and Katherine Frank have argued that Kingsley's "whiteness" enabled her to transcend constructions of gender difference but that "the legacy of sexual oppression paradoxically fostered . . . identification with the subjugated Africans whose lower station facilitated [her] own liberation in Africa."[43] However, as I have illustrated in the context of her perceptions of African women and her definition of racial difference in terms of the objectification of African men, Kingsley's belief in essential difference along lines of both gender and race meant that she perceived "the subjugated Africans" with whom she identified more in terms of racial than gender difference. Kingsley's liberation was inseparable from her ability to identify with imperial power and authority, which remained separate from but could not replace her gendered subjectivity. In this way, although her empathy with Africans arose from her ambiguous position as a woman sharing in imperial power and authority, this was limited to perceptions of racial identity. For Kingsley to empathize with African women constructed as both racially and sexually inferior by imperial and patriarchal discourses would have undermined her own ability to share in imperial power and authority and thus her ability to travel and to legitimate her travels.

It can be argued that the complex ambivalence of constructions of subjectivity over space reflected the negotiation of public and private as well as imperial and patriarchal discursive forma-

tions.[44] To share in imperial, masculine freedom thus correspon
with a public sphere of visibility that was spatially and temporally
delimited, while more personal contact with colonized places and
people corresponded with more feminine, private discourses. The
coexistence of attempted objectivity and subjectivity in Kingsley's
observations and descriptions over space and time similarly highlights the ambivalence of subject and author positionality on her
travels and in her travel writing.

Susan Blake has proposed an alternative interpretation of the
coexistence and complexity of racial superiority and gender inferiority while traveling. She argues that as these are inseparable in
the construction of subjectivity, another basis for authority and
legitimation is necessary and takes the form of class identity. She
compares the Cape to Cairo travel narratives written by Mary Hall
in 1907, Ewart S. Grogan in 1900, and Frank Mellard and Edward
Cholmeley in 1912.[45] Blake identifies clear gender differences between attempts to either overpower or accommodate Africans.
Grogan attempted to physically overpower those he encountered
en route, and Mellard and Cholmeley tried to overpower Africans
within the text, in each case because of an underlying ability
to objectify African subjects. In contrast, Mary Hall attempted to
achieve reciprocity both in her journey and in the text, relating
to Africans as subjects rather than objects. This difference arose
because

> like her male contemporaries, Hall participates in the chivalric struc-
> ture of social relations, but her position in it is split—superior in race
> and class, inferior in gender. . . . The myths of race and gender . . .
> are interdependent. If Africans are savages, unarmed women must
> be vulnerable. Conversely, if woman's power, courtesy, is to work,
> Africans must respond to it; they must be courteous themselves. The
> validation of a woman's strength requires African subjectivity.[46]

Blake's assumption that constructions of race and gender are inseparable conflicts with their evident ambivalence and spatial differentiation in the negotiation of imperial and patriarchal, public
and private spheres while traveling. Such an assumption enables
her to conclude that women travel writers displayed an ambiguous position in the context of imperial legitimation. This notion runs
parallel with the claims of Birkett and Frank that women travel

writers empathized with Africans, but it is substantively different because of her focus on class rather than race or gender:

> the substitution of a sense of class superiority for racial superiority undermines the premises of empire. It transforms the cliché that Africans are childlike from a justification of imperialism to an attitude toward servants. It allows Hall [for example] . . . to acknowledge the social distinctions Africans themselves make and to regard African society as parallel to English. It is her own divided and self-contradictory position as a woman in English society that leads Hall to this implicitly anti-imperialist relationship to Africa.[47]

Constructions of difference exist along lines of, for example, gender, race, and class, and the prioritization of one over another reflects time- and place-specific discursive formations. Rather than artificially isolate one from another, we should see subjectivity as including all of these constructions of difference that vary in their significance and visibility over space and time. The ways in which Kingsley was identified and identified herself as a white, middle-class woman traveling in the context of imperialism reveals the ambivalence and complexity of such constructions, which were inextricably intertwined in her ability to travel and the textual polyphony of her writings about her travels.

MARY KINGSLEY'S IMPERIAL POLITICS

Kingsley advanced a cavalier attitude toward imperial expansion, arguing that

> English government officials have very little and very poor encouragement given them if they push inland and attempt to enlarge the sphere of influence . . . because the authorities at home are afraid other nations will say we are rapacious landgrabbers. Well, we always have been, and they will say it anyhow; and where after all is the harm in it?[48]

She listed reasons for imperial expansion schematically, identifying "religious" and "pressure" reasons, with the latter subdivided into the "external" imperative of war and the "internal" imperatives of

(1) the necessity of supplying restless and ambitious spirits with a field for enterprise during such times as they are not wanted for the defence of their nation in Europe—France's reason for acquiring Africa; (2) population pressure; (3) commercial pressure,[49]

with the final two "pressures" applying to German and English imperialism. For Kingsley, the climate of West Africa meant that imperialism should be primarily oriented toward enlarging markets for surplus production, and she believed that the English were particularly suited to this endeavor, stating "I know that no race of men can battle more gallantly with climate than the English."[50]

Kingsley employed a certain self-conscious femininity when she compared imperial governments. Her charmed, even flirtatious tone enabled her to praise French policy: "Anyone can understand how a woman must admire the deeds of brave men and the backing up of those deeds by a brave Government."[51] Kingsley's national and racial pride is clear when she describes the English as "a truly great people."[52] However, she self-consciously exploits the feminine virtue of "modesty" to veil, but not disguise, her criticisms of the present system of government:

There are three classes of men who are powers to a State—the soldier, the trader, and the scientist. Their efforts, when co-ordinated and directed by the true statesman . . . make a great State. Being English, of course modesty prevents my saying that England is a great State. . . . She . . . will become a great State when she is led by a line of great Statesmen.[53]

Kingsley contrasted the paternal imperialism of the colonist and the trader, likening the former's protection of his "wife and family" to the latter's protection of his trade.[54] This gave rise to a crucial difference in the perception of Africans, because "to the family man the native is a nuisance, sometimes a dangerous one," while the trader's "wealth, prosperity, peace and industry" depended on good relations with "native" customers.[55] Kingsley advocated trade on economic and political grounds, arguing the necessity for expanded markets and for imperial government based on local knowledge. Overall, her political opinions can be summarized by the following statement:

I have attempted to state that the Crown Colony system is unsuited for governing Western Africa, and have attributed its malign influence to its being a system which primarily expresses the opinions of well-intentioned but ill-informed officials at home, instead of being, according to the usual English type of institution, representative of the interests of the people who are governed, and of those who have the largest stake in the countries controlled by it—the merchants and manufacturing classes of England.[56]

CONCLUSION

Kingsley perceived race and gender in terms of essential difference and also perceived these categories as essentially different from each other. However, such perceptions were grounded in the ambivalence of her subjectivity over space as she traveled and as she wrote about her travels. I cited a topographic metaphor at the beginning of this chapter to illustrate her notions that the mountain peaks of Western "civilization" rose above the swamps that Africans both chose to and were forced to inhabit. This provided the context for my discussion of colonized people and places and the ambivalence of Kingsley's subjectivity as a white woman traveling in imperial spheres of influence.

It appears that Kingsley was primarily constructed in terms of her gender subordination while at home but was able to share in racial superiority while traveling because of imperial power and authority. However, what Mills has termed the discourses of difference of race, gender, and class were more complex and ambivalent in their articulation over space than this clear distinction implies. It can be suggested that Kingsley publicly supported imperialism but privately empathized with Africans at least partly because of her split position as both superior and inferior, inside and outside Western discourses of power and authority. However, constructions of gender were also complex and contradictory in their articulation over space, with Kingsley adopting both masculine and feminine voices and codes of conduct on her travels and in her writings.

Kingsley's perceptions of essential difference are undermined by her own contradictory and ambiguous subject position. This becomes clear in her personalization of both places and people, which highlights the tensions of, on the one hand, seeming anti-conquest in the femininity of her subjective identification while, on the other hand, supporting imperialism by attempting to emulate more masculine strategies of objectifying vision. Her political sympathy for traders and her criticisms of the crown colony system of government reflect a desire to reconcile this tension, as she argued that traders should influence policy because of their local knowledge of West Africa and Africans.

In the following chapter, I discuss how Kingsley's political position on her return home led to the coexistence of public and private spheres of influence, and how her gendered subjectivity again seemed to gain preeminence in perceptions of her travels, writings, and politics. Because of the many complex ways in which constructions of subjectivity varied through space as she traveled, I consider how "home" was reconstituted on her return.

NOTES

1. Such ambiguities are stressed by, for example, S. Sheridan, "'Wives and Mothers like Ourselves, Poor Remnants of a Dying Race': Aborigines in Colonial Women's Writing," *Kunapipi* 10 (1988): 76–91. She studies how the racism of white women differed from that of white men and argues that "they construct race difference and relate it to gender difference in specific ways, which on examination reveal the ambiguities of their position as members of the dominant power—but not quite; similarly, the ambiguity of their position as women, shared with Aboriginal women—but not quite" (p. 77).

2. M. H. Kingsley, *Travels in West Africa: Congo, Français, Corisco and Cameroons* (London: Macmillan, 1897), 680. I refer to the implications of this metaphor throughout this chapter.

3. Ibid., 102.

4. J. Duncan, *The City as Text—The Politics of Landscape Interpretation in the Kandyan Kingdom* (Cambridge, England: Cambridge University Press, 1990).

5. Also see A. Blunt, "Mapping Authorship and Authority: Reading Mary Kingsley's Landscape Descriptions," in *Sexual/Textual Colonizations: Women's Colonial and Post-colonial Geographies*, ed. A. Blunt and G. Rose (New York: Guilford Press, forthcoming).

6. Kingsley 1897, xxi.

7. Ibid., 347.

8. Ibid., 177.

9. M. L. Pratt, *Imperial Eyes: Travel Writing and Transculturation* (London: Routledge, 1992).

10. M. H. Kingsley, *West African Studies* (London: Macmillan, 1899).

11. Ibid., 67.

12. Kingsley 1897, 608.

13. M. L. Pratt 1992.

14. Ibid., 213.

15. Ibid.

16. Ibid.

17. Ibid., 214.

18. Ibid. The description Pratt refers to is Kingsley 1897, 338.

19. Kingsley 1897, 338.

20. Ibid.

21. M. L. Pratt 1992, 214.

22. Ibid., 215.

23. Kingsley 1897, 108.

24. Ibid., 594.

25. Ibid., 329.

26. Ibid., 549.

27. Ibid., 550.

28. Ibid., 570.

29. See Chapter 2, this volume, for discussion of Kingsley's accounts of her relationship with the Fans.

30. Kingsley 1897, 574.

31. Ibid., 579.

32. Ibid., 588.

33. Ibid., 594.

34. D. Middleton, *Victorian Lady Travellers* (London: Routledge and Kegan Paul, 1965) describes Kingsley's ascent of Mount Cameroon in the following way: "Through it all runs a sense of strain not apparent in her far more dangerous adventures on the Ogowé. The carriers and servants she took were feckless and faint-hearted and she missed her Fan friends; . . . when she reached the summit it was so swathed in mist that she could see no more than a few feet in front of her. She was, one senses, coming dangerously near that point reached by so many great travellers when danger and hardship cease to be a challenge and become an addiction, when the leader begins to chivy instead of to encourage" (pp. 171–172).

35. D. Birkett, "An Independent Woman in West Africa: The Case of Mary Kingsley" (Ph.D. thesis, University of London, 1987).

36. Kingsley 1897, 653.

37. Kingsley 1899, 373.

38. Ibid., 385.

39. Kingsley 1897, 499.

40. Birkett 1987, 78.

41. Ibid., 118–119.

42. S. Mills, *Discourses of Difference: An Analysis of Women's Travel Writing and Colonialism* (London: Routledge, 1991), 106.

43. K. Frank, "Voyages Out: Nineteenth-Century Women Travelers in Africa," in *Gender, Ideology and Action: Historical Perspectives on Women's Public Lives*, ed. J. Sharistanian (New York: Greenwood, 1986b), 72. Also see Birkett 1987, who argues that "her 'whiteness' gave her opportunities which transcended gender limitations and Mary Kingsley exploited these at the same time as identifying with African subordination. The ambiguities of being defined as a racial superior and sexual subordinate are central to the analysis of her experience in Africa and her position in African affairs" (p. 14).

44. See, for example, Frank 1986b. Also see A. Blunt and G. Rose, "Introduction: Women's Colonial and Post-colonial Geographies," in Blunt and Rose, forthcoming.

45. S. L. Blake, "A Woman's Trek: What Difference Does Gender Make?" *Women's Studies International Forum* 13, 4 (1990): 347–355.

46. Ibid., 353.

47. Ibid., 354.

48. Kingsley 1897, 674.

49. Kingsley 1899, 291–292.

50. Ibid., 302.

51. Ibid., 267.

52. Ibid., 297.

53. Ibid.

54. Ibid., 294.

55. Ibid., 295.

56. Ibid., 314.

Return

RECONSTITUTING HOME

"Home" is constructed in an arbitrary, retrospective way while the traveler is away, and, by necessity, "home" changes on the traveler's return.[1] It can be argued that travels themselves exist only when bounded by departure and return and are thus similarly retrospective. The significance of such a dialectical relationship between "home" and away for imperial women travel writers lay in their own perceptions of "home" and how they were perceived by others on their return. In this chapter I discuss the ways in which women travel writers, specifically, Mary Kingsley, were constructed primarily in terms of gender difference, and how this paralleled but differed from such constructions prior to departure. I hope to illuminate the coexistence of public and private spheres of activity and influence by focusing on reader responses to Kingsley's publications articulated by reviews; her political roles evident in her articles, letters, and lectures; and more personal perceptions of her individuality as expressed in obituaries. Initially, however, I illustrate the familiarization and defamiliarization of the two worlds of "home" and away in the writings of Kingsley.

At several points in *Travels in West Africa*, Kingsley juxtaposed "home" and away in an incongruous way that highlights her unique position as traveling subject mediating these spheres. This juxtaposition is particularly evident in terms of the infrastructure of traveling itself; for example, she wrote that "changing at Lagos Bar throws changing at Clapham Junction into the shade"[2] and familiarized fetish by stating that

> you white men will say, "Why go on believing in him then?" but that
> is an idea that does not enter the African mind. I might just as well

say "Why do you go on believing in the existence of hansom cabs," because one hansom cab driver malignantly fails to take you where you want to go, or fails to arrive in time to catch a train you wished to catch.[3]

Traveling in West Africa was both unfamiliar and incongruously familiar, and the ways in which travel is inseparable from ways of knowing is translated onto Kingsley's projected perceptions of home:

It's Africa all over; presenting one with familiar objects when one least requires them, like that razor in the heart of Gorilla-land; and unfamiliar, such as elephants and buffaloes when you are out for a quiet stroll armed with a butterfly net, to say nothing of snakes in one's bed and scorpions in one's boots and sponge. One's view of life gets quite distorted; I don't believe I should be in the least surprised to see a herd of hippo stroll on to the line out of one of the railway tunnels of Notting Hill Gate station. West Africa is undoubtedly bad for one's mind.[4]

PUBLIC AND PRIVATE
RECONSTRUCTIONS OF "HOME"

To travel "home" and to write about traveling from the perspective of "home" points up the reflexivity of such constructions and the immanence of a traveling and writing subject mediating spatial difference. Here I contrast the public and private activity and perceptions of Kingsley to illustrate the ambivalence of her subjectivity on her return. I discuss reader responses to her publications to locate her political platform in the context of public recognition. I also discuss her individuality and how constructions of private spheres of influence came to be publicly articulated in articles, reviews, and obituaries.

Reader Responses
to Women's Travel Writing

Kingsley returned from her second journey to West Africa in November 1895, and the earliest references to her travels appeared in the first week of December. For example, the *Times* wrote about her desire to downplay potential sensationalism, stating that "Miss

Kingsley refused to relate any gorilla stories, saying that too much doubt was cast upon all such accounts by the public."[5] The following day, a longer article published in the *Daily Telegraph* located her within but clearly different from a masculine tradition of exploration. The femininity of Kingsley as "heroine" established her as distinctive:

> The latest African novelty is seen in the return of an English lady from the most surprising and courageous adventures, undergone without any assistance from the "Creature Man," and in a portion of the Continent recently regarded as practically inaccessible.[6]

Such independence established her as primarily eccentric, as shown by the paternalist tone adopted to depict her travels through Fan territory: "What a country for an English Miss to traverse alone, where the only place of burial for the defunct is inside of his neighbour"[7] and the conclusion that

> Yes! anything seems possible in Africa; yet almost more wonderful than the hidden marvels of that Dark Continent are the qualities of heart and mind which could carry a lonely English lady through such experiences as Miss Kingsley has "manfully" borne.[8]

Gender and nationality seem inseparable, and the construction of an "English lady" seems to epitomize notions of appropriate feminine conduct transgressed by Kingsley. In response to this article, Kingsley emphasized the help she received from traders while traveling and downplayed her achievements, caricaturing herself in terms of gender inferiority:

> I did not do anything except things I had better have left alone—without the assistance of the superior sex. . . . I just puddled round obscure corners and immersed myself in catastrophes.[9]

Despite such early interest, the most sustained coverage of Kingsley's travels followed the publication of *Travels in West Africa* and, particularly, *West African Studies.* From a poststructuralist perspective, texts are processes of signification articulated only through reading because "meaning has no effective existence outside of its realization in the mind of a reader."[10] For Jonathan Culler, reader response is influenced by the sign systems that readers conventionally apply to texts through their, in this case, literary "competence."[11] This relates to the ideological construction of literature, as readers' responses are constrained by their ability to perceive, read, and interpret as discursively constructed subjects. Kingsley's publications were widely read,[12] but the only way to ascertain individual readings of her texts lies in published reviews. These readings were themselves likely to be influential in enabling and constraining further interpretations because of their textually fixed authority. Reviews were printed in national and regional newspapers, women's periodicals, and more specialized, imperial journals such as *West Africa* and the *West African News and Mining Review*. I focus on how these reviews constructed Kingsley as a gendered subject on her return.

Reviews of *Travels in West Africa* focused on the novelty of a woman traveler, while reviews of *West African Studies* focused on the book's style and content. The studio photograph of Kingsley taken around 1897 clearly conveys the feminine image she was concerned to present when *Travels in West Africa* was published. The *Scottish Geographical Magazine* described *Travels in West Africa* as

> quite a new departure in African literature, and, after reading it, one is not surprised at its popularity and extensive sale, for such a sprightly, interesting, vivid, and in some respects audacious, account of travels in Africa, it has never been our lot to read—and the author a lady![13]

The codes of conduct for women travelers prior to departure related primarily to appearance and behavior in the face of potential dangers. After stating that "female curiosity apparently has no limits," the *New York Times* characterized Kingsley as conforming to feminine standards: "The lady for hard work . . . has no liking for bloomers or any masculine garb, but the highest opinion of the advantages of petticoats."[14]

In the following review, Kingsley's femininity in the face of adversity was established by her appearance and emotions:

> Civilisation clung more or less to her skirts at Cape Coast and other settlements; and it was with relief that Miss Kingsley re-embarked to fall in love with the wild beauty of Fernando Po, and to explore the Ogowé, a mighty stream watering Congo Français.[15]

Title illustrations of the West African News *and* West Africa, *depicting Britannia ruling supreme over West Africa.*

To say that Kingsley "fell in love" with a landscape, to describe the Ogowé as "a mighty stream," and for another review to refer to Kingsley's journey as "her walk"[16] minimized her achievements compared with a masculine tradition of exploration.

To locate a feminine subject in dangerous situations has the potential both to undermine and reinforce such constructions according to the tone adopted and the behavior depicted. In a review of *Travels in West Africa*, an amused tone downplays the dangers encountered, conveying the image of an eccentric, feminine subject rather than the control and bravery that might be expected from white men establishing imperial power and authority:

Mary Kingsley in 1897. Courtesy of the Royal Commonwealth Society Library, London.

It is not possible to follow the adventurous author through all her perilous situations, and readers must go to the book itself to see how she warded off the attack of a crocodile, tumbled into the water out of a canoe, escaped many other dangers, and was extricated from several awkward predicaments.[17]

Rather than displaying the physical, administrative, or intellectual skill of masculine explorers, Kingsley overcame danger through her more feminine behavioral virtues; she

carried a merry heart with her, and the success of this good medicine is shown by the way in which she escaped serious consequences in the course of her extended travels through the most unhealthy parts of Africa.[18]

Or as a review of *West African Studies* put it, "Her unfailing high spirits were a priceless possession to a wanderer in the jungle of countries where malignant melancholy is frequently epidemic."[19]

Several reviews of *West African Studies* characterized Kingsley as an individual transcending conventional notions of feminine subjectivity. A tone of wonderment describing "her venturesomeness and contempt of danger"[20] undermined notions of appropriate feminine conduct. She was further described as being "as plucky in her way as the masculine explorer,"[21] and one account said that "as a politician Miss Kingsley is vigorous and determined, as a traveler she is shrewd and anecdotal."[22] In addition, reviews of *West African Studies* were more likely to locate Kingsley's writings within a broader tradition of travel writing. Overall, her writings were judged favorably, as by the following statement: "No living traveller is half so amusing to read, and very few are half as instructive."[23]

Unlike the reviews of *Travels in West Africa*, those of *West African Studies* highlighted its form, style, and content, which were perceived as inseparable. This represented a movement away from the curiosity value of *Travels in West Africa* to the more substantive value of *West African Studies*, supporting claims that travel writing often takes two contrasting forms. The inseparability of form, style, and content is illustrated by a description of *West African Studies* as "rollicking fun and solid information,"[24] but interpretations ranged from high praise to derision. I am particularly interested in how the reader responses expressed in reviews of *West African Studies* revealed and reproduced perceptions of gendered subjectivity.

Most reviews criticized Kingsley's style of writing, although some seemed paternal in excusing faults and some praised her style because of its femininity. The harshest criticisms appeared in the *Glasgow Herald*:

> Miss Kingsley's faults as a writer, which did less serious damage to her narrative of travel, are here very tiresomely and sometimes very offensively apparent. She is extremely diffuse and irrelevant; has no notion of orderly arrangement; and, worst of all, she perpetually insists on being funny after the manner of the newest humorists. The consequence is that her pages often read like a bad imitation of "Three Men in a Boat." It is a pity that Miss Kingsley has not tried to write in a more ladylike manner, because when she pleases she can write well enough. She has the skill of vivid and picturesque description.[25]

In contrast, the most fulsome, indeed hyperbolic, praise for *West African Studies* celebrated her style precisely for its essential femininity:

> The fresh, vigorous, breezy style of the writer, as spontaneous and as refreshing as a moorland stream that bubbles with laughter as it leaps over difficulties or gets round them somehow, has a special charm about it. . . . Of course she can be discursive. How could a lady, so crammed full of her subject, so light-hearted and gay in her manner and yet so earnest, too, be otherwise? But it is a discursiveness that lights up with bright touches of humour what in the hands of many male writers—nay, most—would be dull and heavy.[26]

Most reviews, however, lay between these extremes, for example tolerating her "countless unnecessary digressions" because "she is frankly so unconventional, and takes so keen a pleasure in her own flippancies";[27] describing it as "undoubtedly a very readable book, though the chaffy and somewhat flippant style of the authoress becomes a little tiresome";[28] and viewing the "real power" of her description as "infinitely preferable to literary polish."[29]

Kingsley's "knowledge" was discussed most extensively in the context of fetish, while her alternative plan was little more than referred to. Her direct observations were praised, but her political proposals did not receive the same level of legitimation through critique. The "fact"-based nature of her discussion of fetish was stressed, and she was seen to possess "a consuming zeal for knowledge and a genuine passion for facts."[30] Although the *Daily News* referred to "the extent, variety, and reasoned order of her knowledge,"[31] the *Standard* stated that "the effect of her essays [on fetish] is to confuse the mind."[32] A clear distinction was made between the value of her observations and interpretations; for example, the *Glasgow Herald* stated that

> her remarks on the essential nature and origin of what is loosely called fetishism do not strike us as being very profound or helpful, but as an observer she has many interesting facts to tell.[33]

Finally, *West African Studies* was criticized for appealing neither to specialist nor general readers, with her style undermining the value of the content by not conforming to scientific standards. On the one hand, the *Echo* criticized the disparity between general interest—at least for male readers—and more specialized concerns:

> After the first hundred and fifty pages in which he [the reader] has revelled in racy anecdote and swift artistic sketches, he becomes involved in disquisitions scientific and political which, though undoubtedly of great value to the specialist, scarcely carry the reader forward like the opening chapters of the book.[34]

On the other hand, the *Yorkshire Post* argued that while Kingsley's accounts of fetish

> will interest the general reader, the student of such subjects is not as a rule the person who cares much for the kind of discursive chatter which Miss Kingsley pours out with such astonishing volubility. Still, she has looked at her subject on the spot, and that is more than can sometimes be said for learned writers on topics of this kind.[35]

Overall, initial responses to *Travels in West Africa* reflected interest in the travels of a woman and thus with Kingsley as author, but the reviews of *West Africa Studies* were more concerned with form, style, and content. Clearly, however, this distinction was blurred, as shown by the underlying significance of perceptions of gender difference. Before discussing Kingsley's political influence and whether this promoted changing perceptions of her writings,

I conclude with a quotation from the *New York Times* review of *Travels in West Africa*, which reflects reader responses more broadly over time:

> The author's sex has probably had something to do with the interest awakened but not this alone could have carried the book on so successful a career. The vital merits of it have been the real source of its popularity. Miss Kingsley had an adventurous journey, and she showed remarkable courage and resources in meeting emergencies. But the book is unconventional in many ways. It abounds in humor, fresh information, bright descriptions, originality of view, and is written in an animated style.[36]

Public Politics

Kingsley was an outspoken political figure on specific issues and on imperialism in general. In this section I focus on the extent to which her distinctive position as a woman traveler and author influenced her views, her means of expression, and their reception. I then discuss the coexistence of this public role with her attempts to fulfill familial duty constructed as feminine and public perceptions of her more private personality. At this stage, however, I outline Kingsley's political position, her public roles in "society" and in public speaking, and the paradoxical way in which private correspondence underlay her public influence to discuss the complex ambivalence of constructions of gender difference in a conventionally masculine sphere of activity.

Kingsley was positioned both inside and outside society and culture not only while she traveled in West Africa but also on her return to Britain. Her consciousness of this status is most evident in her references to "society" and to the general public as a whole, reflecting the distinctive ambiguities of her subject position on the margins of "home" and away. Her ambiguous status underlay and facilitated her criticisms of certain forms of imperialism. For example, in an undated letter to Alice Stopford Green, Kingsley's frustration is clear:

> There are a lot of people here who unless you can pour melted butter over their national vanity—it's nothing else—think you don't care about your country. I don't care about them for they have never been any use to any sort of country they belong to.[37]

This is echoed in a letter to John Holt:

> The general public seems to hunger and thirst after nothing but praise of England, and they call that Imperialism. They would never have had an Empire to intoxicate themselves over if the making of it had been in their hands.[38]

Similarly, Kingsley criticized "this smug, self-satisfied, lazy, sanctimonious, 'Times' believing England."[39]

Kingsley saw herself as detached from the conventions and constrictions of "society," criticized "these fashionable smart foolish folk here who bore[,] weary and disgust me with their ignorance[,] conceit and airs of grandly good intentions,"[40] and lamented the limitations imposed by notions of feminine conduct whereby "woman-like I get tired of holding my tongue as I have to do up here."[41] She saw herself as an outsider, as she most graphically expressed in a letter to Lady MacDonald, in which her frustration with the superficiality and hypocrisy of socially acceptable behavior is evident:

> I have been watching the game here, just as I watch in Africa, as an outsider—and it is not half so good a game to watch. I was yesterday at two At Homes and a dinner, at every one of which I saw people who had abused their hosts up hill and down dale or who their hosts had abused ditto. Yet there they were all together smiling and calling each other by their Christian names and so on—it all seems to me silly and sinful and it[']s uncommon dull.[42]

Kingsley's dislike of "society" duty heightened her identification with Africa and Africans, as shown by her statements that "we Africans are not fit for decent society"[43] and "Give me the West African bush and the calm of a cannibal town!"[44] The fixity of and the distinction between "home" and away are thus undermined, and from a distance and her position of gender subordination, Kingsley seems most able to identify with the racial subordination of Africans perceived as others. Not only was "home" constructed through traveling and returning, but on her return Kingsley's inability to feel "at home" and her references to West Africa as "home" reveal the destabilization of both "home" and away.

Kingsley's political influence was underpinned by her marginal position as a traveler personally able to bridge the social and spatial distance between colonized and colonizing worlds. This was a distinctive position, and following the publicity surrounding her travels and the publication of *Travels in West Africa*, "this early picture of her as a maverick traveller gave her the opportunity to espouse highly individualistic views and remain quite consistent in her public appeal."[45] More than this, however, her subject position was marginal because of constructions of gendered subjectivity. It is notable that Kingsley perceived such marginality as a source of strength, enabling her distinctive voice to be heard. For example, she wrote to John Holt that "you men will be men. A Frenchman would not listen to an Englishman talking to him about how to manage his colonies but he don't mind a woman doing so."[46] Furthermore, what suggests patriarchal domination instead seemed to possess subversive potential for Kingsley: "Every bit of solid good work I have done has been through a man, and I get more and more fond of doing things this way. It leaves me a free hand to fight with."[47] Kingsley further exploited her gendered subjectivity in her relationship and influence with Liverpool traders, caricaturing herself as their "maiden aunt."[48] Despite such notions of marginal strength and the potential for resistance, these were constrained within the strategic parameters of public politics, whereby Kingsley felt "as if I were always playing games up here with these people— it amuses but underneath I hate it, but I must do it for the stakes are men[']s lives."[49] Kingsley played political games on a number of levels, including the public sphere of lectures, press coverage, and publications; the official sphere of the Colonial Office; and the private, unofficial spheres of many individuals and companies with widely ranging interests. In what follows I focus on how Kingsley moved within and between these spheres as a woman in the context of patriarchal discourses of gender difference.

Following the publication of *Travels in West Africa*, Kingsley increasingly moved away from a focus on specific issues such as liquor traffic to more general political proposals epitomized by her "Alternative Plan" in *West African Studies*. Her campaign for the removal of the hut tax in Sierra Leone represented a transition from highly specific to more general concerns. She privately argued that

> West Africa my Lord is a mess, and I feel certain they will make it a
> bigger mess still by merely throwing in a lot of money, without hav-

ing anyone there who understands how to manage it—and by trying to tax the natives in ways those natives regard as unfair and oppressive—I have no objection to the native being taxed, it is merely a matter of method,[50]

and she referred to the hut tax as a "criminally ignorant hasty grab for money."[51] Kingsley publicly expressed her opinions in a letter to the *Spectator*, stating that "taxing a man's individual possession is a violation of his idea of property."[52] She introduced her argument as a response to an article that did not refer to the hut tax and stressed the need for effective and efficient imperial rule.[53]

In her private correspondence, Kingsley was vehement in her opposition to "jubilee imperialism,"

that is conceited beyond words, that gets pains in it now and then from Mr Kipling with his "white man's burden" but which won't work at facts and shrinks from criticism like an old lady from a black beetle. It is the black man's burden that wants singing for the poor wretch has to put up with a lot of windy headed fads and foolishness no good to him or the white man and a jest for the gods.[54]

In another letter to the *Spectator*, Kingsley contrasted

our commercial expansion in the days of Elizabeth . . . marked by an intense love of knowledge of the minor details . . . [with] our colonial, or emigrant, expansion of the age of Victoria . . . marked by no such love of detailed knowledge; in its place there is emotionalism.[55]

She proceeded to condemn "that emotionalism I so deeply detest and distrust [as] windy-headed brag and self-satisfied ignorance,"[56] and she was supported by an editorial note that stated,

[We] trust her plea for patience, thoroughness, and clear and clean intention, as against sloppiness, mental and moral, and vague well-meaningness, will not pass unheeded.[57]

Kingsley's opinions of imperialism were inseparable from her support of trade in West Africa. I outline this allegiance in the context of her need to legitimate her political involvement and her desire to consolidate a trading lobby and to identify its leader. Following her direct contact with traders overseas, Kingsley advocated

the position of trading companies based in Liverpool. On her return, Kingsley traveled literally and metaphorically between clearly
characterized places. In so doing, she constructed them as spatially
and politically distinct and created a position of authority for herself as a traveler within and between them. Kingsley thus traveled
not only between Britain and West Africa but also on her return,
so that "home" was more transient than fixed. For example, she
wrote to E. D. Morel that

> Liverpool as Liverpool sits on the fence. I love Liverpool but I do think
> it artful—just a little too obviously artful at times. Manchester is more
> reckless, stands up to its man . . . as the Times set now say "Liverpool
> can do no harm in Miss Kingsley's eyes"—certainly I will never let
> London know if it does.[58]

The ways in which both public and private spheres were important and inseparable in underpinning Kingsley's political position are well illustrated by her desire to consolidate the interests
of the Liverpool traders into an effective political lobby. She referred
to the mercantile community as "disgracefully unorganised,"[59] perceiving the need for strong leadership. Her opinions of personal
power were most vividly expressed in a letter she wrote to Alice
Stopford Green while sailing for South Africa:

> Do not dream of in any way sacrificing yourself for any cause—I am
> not saying causes are not worth it but merely that they cannot be
> helped by sacrifice of that kind. Set yourself to gain personal power—
> don't grab the reins of power—but [while] they are laying on the
> horses neck, quietly get them into your hands and drive.[60]

This implies a desire for effective but essentially covert control with
more private than public influence. Kingsley's main channel for
exercising such influence was her prolific letter writing, most
notably to John Holt, and her political patronage of two young jour-
nalists, Stephen Gwynn and E. D. Morel, whose work she recommended to editors and publishers.

Kingsley's letter writing was often initiated through a female
contact. For example, her first, indirect, communication with John
Holt was to accept his wife's invitation to address the Highgate
Literary and Scientific Institute.[61] In other letters Kingsley seems

to have used feminine influence in the informal, private sphere of social introductions, for example, inviting Mrs. Holt to meet Alice Stopford Green.[62]

Kingsley felt a sense of duty in supporting the position of traders, but seemed more at ease in creating unofficial rather than official contacts. For example, her tone is despondent in a letter written to John Holt in May 1898:

> Alas I am sick at heart over the whole thing. You know I have stood up for all I am worth for trade and the trader. I have taken up the position accident gave me, just that I might use that position to teach people the importance of trade and the trader, and what[']s the good. I hate lecturing and writing letters to papers and articles in magazines and above all I hate being amiable to people who say "Oh we must teach those horrid brutes a lesson—they must not be allowed to think that just because they fight we will let them have their way." That's what I had the Pleasure of hearing yesterday from a high official.[63]

Her private attempts to gain public influence were most graphic in her relationship with John Holt. She wrote: "What I want to see done Mr Holt is a Liverpool School of Politics formed for controlling African legislation. . . . Now you are the man who can do it."[64] In her following letter, she instructed John Holt to write to the *Spectator* in support of her letter opposing the hut tax:

> Now what I want you to do is to write a letter to the Spectator . . . , short because long ones get back, pitch into me as much as you please, but go for the folly of the hut tax. . . . The letter ought to reach the Spectator by Tuesday next, namely be posted tonight to the Editor of the Spectator. . . . I need not say that if it *does not suit you* to write it pray do not, but if you want the tax off you must strike while the iron is *hot*, and we shall get it done. *I have written a letter to the editor about the possibility of having a letter from you.*[65]

It seems that her contact with John Holt led Kingsley to exaggerate her influence among Liverpool traders as a general body. Even though Kingsley was often successful in their manipulation, her position as a woman constrained her within private, personal circles of influence. She attempted to achieve public recognition of West African politics rather than public recognition for herself, and this was clearly shown in her concern that West Africa was being increasingly overshadowed by South Africa. Her instructions to John Holt were echoed in a letter to E. D. Morel in which she wrote,

> Cannot you write a letter pointing out how misguided and tiresome I am, and what a blessed thing Imperial control is if it is altered so that its own mother would not know it etc, in fact any mortal thing you like, for I am sure West Africa's one chance of getting attended to is in gaining publicity in the press.[66]

She described her primary role as publicizing West African affairs:

> I do my uttermost to create [a] reading public. I try to educate people to look for West African news in the papers. I do not care whether the news goes with me or against me. I want it there . . . because I honestly believe that the great mass of information on West Africa must make up for the truth and until the truth is known to the general public the GP will be content to let things slide there.[67]

Kingsley's support of Liverpool traders bridged publicly political and more privately personal spheres of influence because she believed that the traders' local knowledge and experience should be channeled into policymaking. References to a "Liverpool sect" at this time relate primarily to the ideals of Kingsley, John Holt, and E. D. Morel and can be summarized in the following way:

> It called on all having relations with West Africa to take note of the existing and traditional systems there. It desired that the West African should continue under British rule to be a landholder with security of tenure, an agriculturalist and trader. It advocated an increased study of West Africa, and demanded that time should be allowed for a gradual development from within the region, deprecating the swift and immediate introduction of European norms and formulae which not only dislocated the African polity but also made hybrids of the inhabitants.[68]

However, the direct political influence of the "Liverpool sect" was limited because

> its major proposals lacked any solid economic backing or wide public appeal. It was handicapped by the sublime opportunism of other Liverpool traders and by the institutionalized indifference of the British Chambers of Commerce.[69]

Kingsley gained personal publicity with audiences as well as readers because of the many lectures she gave. Her direct contact with people highlights her perceived detachment from them. For example, she wrote to Alice Stopford Green: "Do you see the nasty things they say about me at the Women's Writers Dinner for dropping my g's—just as if it were not all I could do to hold on to the h's,"[70] suggesting that the way she spoke identified her as belonging to a lower class. She lectured to diverse audiences, preferring northern industrial towns where "I know how much to explain to half an inch"[71] and caricaturing

> these literary and scientific Institutions [which] amuse me much—they always write and inform you they don't want science and literature. . . . What they want is "something bright and amusing and magic lantern slides." I have at moments grave doubts as to whether the Times and the Spectator are right when they say the British Public insists on being taken seriously."[72]

Kingsley viewed her lectures in pragmatic terms and wrote to her lecture agent that "English manufacturing towns I am personally fond of—for the rest every pound means five miles in West Africa next time out."[73]

Kingsley's lectures were diverse in content to suit her audiences. After her death it was noted that she

> was the only lady who has delivered an address to the Manchester Chamber of Commerce during its hundred years of existence; I think it is a proof of the respect and admiration with which her abilities were regarded in commercial circles, that she should have been asked to address a meeting of businessmen on matters concerning commercial interests.[74]

In contrast, she spoke on "The Trials of a Tropical Traveller" in 1897 at the Highgate Literary and Scientific Institute, where

> although she recited in a calm, unemotional style, and with an absence of anything like dramatic effect, Miss Kingsley yet managed to draw a sufficiently vivid picture of a traveller's life in Africa as to thoroughly impress her hearers with a sense of the dangers and difficulties that beset the stranger, especially a woman, in that comparatively little known region; and looking upon her placid features, and listening to the quiet tones of her voice, it seemed incredible that so slight a frame

could have endured such hardships and faced such dangers as she did, and which, happily, it is given to few women to go through.[75]

In 1898 she gave a lecture at the Cheltenham Ladies College that was reprinted in their magazine. Her humor is as evident as in her written accounts and is best illustrated by her references to her unmarried status and how she could manipulate interest in this while she was traveling:

> I may confide to any spinster who is here present and who feels inclined to take up the study of [Africans] that she will be perpetually embarrassed by enquiries of, Where is your husband? not, Have you one? or anything like that, which you could deal with, but, Where is he? I must warn her not to say she has not got one, I have tried it, and it only leads to more appalling questions still. I think that it is more advisable to say you are searching for him, and then you locate him away in the direction in which you wish to travel; this elicits help and sympathy.[76]

In this lecture Kingsley most eloquently and vividly expressed her homesickness for West Africa. One passage in particular highlights her wistful tone, her powers of more than visual description, and her sense of detachment on her return "home":

> The charm of West Africa is a painful one. It gives you pleasure to fall under it when you are out there, but when you are back here, it gives you pain, by calling you. It sends up before your eyes a vision of a wall of dancing, white, rainbow-gemmed surf playing on a shore of yellow sand before an audience of stately cocoa palms, *or* of a great mangrove-walled bronze river, or of a vast forest cathedral, and you hear, *nearer* to you than the voices of the people round you, *nearer* than the roar of the city traffic, the sound of that surf that is beating on the shore down there, and the sound of the wind talking in the hard palm leaves, and the thump of the natives' tom-toms, or the cry of the parrots passing over the mangrove swamps in the evening time—and everything that is round you grows poor and thin in the face of that vision, and you want to go back to the Coast that is calling you, saying, as the African says to the departing soul of his dying friend, "Come back, this is your home."[77]

These examples[78] illustrate in different ways how Kingsley was primarily identified, and also identified herself, in terms of gendered subjectivity. In addition, her lectures show the ways in which she felt personally inadequate on a literal as well as figurative public platform, remarking to Macmillan, for example, "Why people . . . want me to lecture when I do it so badly passes me."[79] Her different audiences reflected the diverse interpretations of Kingsley's travels, and the ways in which she adjusted the content of her lectures according to her audiences reflected her awareness of their differences. However, at times she was on public display in social contexts in which she was unable to change sensationalist perceptions of her character and travels. For example, at a dinner party held in her honor in Edinburgh,

> I felt highly inclined to ask them why they did not ask the lady who dives through the roof at the Aquarium and the female lion tamers. The side of me they pretend to admire is no higher than this sort of thing. "Oh, Miss Kingsley *how* many *men* did you kill?" *I* who never lost a porter.[80]

Private Personality

On her return, Kingsley was active in both public and private spheres, illustrating the ambivalence of constructions both of these spheres and of gendered subjectivity. As well as laying the foundations for her publicly political position, her private correspondence was also a channel for self-reflection. I discuss this below in conjunction with the many published obituaries of Kingsley to highlight the ways in which her life, travels, and writings were ultimately attributed to her highly individual but at all times clearly gendered subjectivity.

Kingsley questioned her identity as a traveler and a travel writer, illustrating the conflicts arising from the coexistence of private and public spheres of activity and representation. For example, in a letter to Lady MacDonald, she wrote,

> I am really beginning to think that the traveler—properly so called— the person who writes a book and gets his FRGS etc., is a peculiar sort of animal only capable of seeing a certain set of things and always seeing them in the same way, and you and me are not of this species somehow. What are we to call ourselves? I have been wading through many volumes of travel lately, among them Mr Robinson's; he went to Okano . . . this side up, fragile keep dry and all that sort of thing you know. Well! save for the names of the places, he

might as far as local colour goes have gone to Korea or Cumberland. ... Still I do not reproach them but sympathize with them, deeply, now I have had a turn at writing an African book myself, and I have come to the decision that it is the greatest mistake to write a book about a place you have been to. ... personal experiences get in your way sadly. The amount of expurgation my journals have required has been awful.[81]

Kingsley's "personal experiences" on her return to Britain were oriented around a sense of duty to family and friends. Tensions between this duty to others and her desire for self-fulfillment were most clearly expressed by her sense of personal inadequacy and melancholy. She wrote to Dennis Kemp that "I have always a feeling of responsibility" and looked back to "the dreadful gloom of all my life until I went to Africa"; in her family duties, she wrote "I tried my best, and I know I failed, for my mother's sufferings were terrible, and my brother's health is now far from what I should wish."[82] Her perceived freedom to travel depended on her sense of family responsibility:

When I shall get out to West Africa I am not sure—because of my Brother. He is the only person who is a duty to me so I cannot leave him for my own pleasure, but apart from him I am wearying to be away for life up here tires without interesting me.[83]

However, her sense of responsibility extended beyond her brother to a wider sphere of friends and relations, as shown by her letters to Mrs. Holt:

One of my mother's oldest friends became very ill and I had to be with her till she died the day after Xmas day, meanwhile the son of another friend a boy of 18 got influenza ... he died and she went mad and remains so. I have had to come home from her.[84]

In her following letter, she mentions an uncle "very ill and very, very tiresome and I have got to go down to his house so as to let his daughter off duty."[85]

Kingsley recognized the contrast between her personal doubts and public assurance, describing herself as "a very tortured soul."[86] Her public role seemed to mask profound insecurities:

> The best part of me is ... doubt, and self-distrust and melancholy,
> and heartache over other people. Why should I show it to people I
> don't care for and don't know? I put on armour and coruscating wit
> ... when I go out to battle.[87]

Her sense of inadequacy compared with other people was particularly pronounced in her friendships with women. For example, she wrote to Sir Alfred Lyall that his wife was

> so restful and pleasant to me whose home is in the valley of the
> shadow of death. I thought when I left Cambridge I had left that val-
> ley, but it was an error. It is evidently my home and I must reconcile
> myself to it, build my shimbec there and settle down, but it does me
> good to come out of it into Lady Lyall's sunshine.[88]

Her melancholy is also clear in a letter to Alice Stopford Green:

> You don't know the sort of background of wretchedness that is be-
> hind things in my mind—that knowledge that all the people I have
> slaved for have never given me any gratitude and that there is another
> set of people for whom I have done *nothing* for whom I can *never*
> do *anything* who lavish on me kindness I do not deserve and then I
> see there must be something wrong in me, that these latter set, among
> which you are preeminent, must be under some delusion about me.
> ... I should be very miserable without you so perhaps the less I dwell
> on my innate unworthiness the better.[89]

Kingsley's melancholy was often closely tied to her physical health. The previous quotation followed her statement that "I am in a nasty, fractious, naughty, miserable, lonely state of mind, but it will pass off when I am stronger."[90] Kingsley's physical strength was in turn closely tied to her inability to enjoy England, as expressed to Lady MacDonald:

> I am low in mind, principally from being low in my health with ever-
> lasting colds and headaches but also from having sort of lost the power
> of enjoying life in England.[91]

Compared with her apparently excellent health while traveling in a region infamous for its climate, Kingsley seemed sensitive to the British climate, suffering frequent colds, influenza, and rheumatism as well as neuralgia and headaches. In contrast to the lack of references to her health in her travel books, her correspondence on her return to Britain was punctuated by comments such as "I am terribly weak and tired"[92] and "I have been ill this week with one of my bad colds, and much depressed."[93]

The only time that Kingsley complained of ill health in Africa was while nursing in South Africa. In her last letter to Alice Stopford Green she wrote from Cape Town that "My chest is still wrong—but do not worry about me."[94] This final letter includes Kingsley's most vivid reflections on her personality and the differences between "home" and away that she bridged by traveling and returning:

> I am down in the muck of life again—whether I shall come up out of this like I came up out of West Africa and associated with thinking people I don't know. It is a personally risky game I am playing here and it is doubtful—one nurse and an orderly who have only been on two days are down themselves—but if I do not believe me my dear Lady I am eternally grateful to you for all your kindness and your infinite toleration and thoughtfulness for me. I who was and am and never shall be anything but a mucker—all this work here—the stink the washing the enemas the bed pans the blood is my world, not London Society politics and that gallery into which I so strangely wandered—into which I don't care a hairpin if I don't wander again. Take care of yourself—you who can do so much more than I in what St Loe [Strachey] calls the *haut politique* and remember it is the haut politique that makes me have to catch large powerful family men by the tails of their night shirts at midnight stand over them when they are stinking—tie up their jaws when they are dead—5 or 6 jaws a night I have had of late to tie up—*Dam* the haut politique.[95]

*   *   *

Mary Kingsley died—alone, as was her wish,[96]—on June 3, 1900. Many obituaries were printed in national and regional newspapers, traders' journals, and women's periodicals. Most emphasized Kingsley's character and appearance, illustrating that her subjectivity was constructed primarily along lines of gender difference on her return "home."

Although some obituaries did not explicitly praise Kingsley's feminine virtues, they often implicitly reproduced them, as shown by a description of her as a singularly lovable and original personality . . . a quiet retiring person absolutely unconcerned about herself, and ceaselessly occupied in doing service to others. She could feel for communities or parties without losing her sympathy for any individual, and though she was constantly engaged in controversy over the most contentious issues, personal enmity was apparently unknown to her.[97]

The *Times* described her as "a sincere and conscientious seeker after the truth," with "a modest and retiring disposition"[98] and the *Athenaeum* listed

the variety of her richly endowed nature, her commanding intellect, her keen insight, her originality, her tenderness, her simplicity, her absolute freedom from cant or pretence, her delightful humour, her extraordinary grasp of the problems, physical, ethnological, or political, to which as occasion arose she turned her attention.[99]

In addition, her "sane and states*man*like views on African questions"[100] and her "analytical, scientific mind"[101] were praised.

However, most assessments of Kingsley's character focused on her gendered subjectivity, revealing less about her travels, writing, and politics than about contemporary constructions of femininity. E. D. Morel wrote,

That she, a weak woman labouring under the many disadvantages which under such circumstances her sex necessarily entailed, should have succeeded in effecting so much is surely a lesson to every one of us,[102]

but most obituaries perceived her gender in essentialist terms, particularly relating to appropriate behavior, sentiments, and appearance. However, despite many attempts to portray Kingsley as inherently feminine, these were often qualified by complex and ambivalent constructions of gender difference because of, first, the ways in which she was regarded as bridging distinctions between masculine and feminine characteristics and, second, the perceived differences between Kingsley and other women.

Kingsley's death promoted portrayals of self-sacrifice and feminine duty that elevated her to the stature of a heroine such as Florence Nightingale.[103] She was seen as superior to other nurses because

in "the plague" of fashionable ladies who infested South Africa at a time when only conscientious, practical and sensible nurses were required, the very name of Mary Kingsley will appear as a bird of paradise above a flock of screaming, chattering magpies.[104]

Although her death was seen as appropriately feminine, her life was seen as more ambivalent; for example, an obituary in the *Lady* stated that

> she died at last a woman's death in a centre of civilisation, but perhaps that will only strengthen people's memories to recall that she had lived like a man in strange countries where civilisation had not gained the mastery.[105]

It seems paradoxical that at the same time as Kingsley was seen to possess both feminine and masculine qualities and to transcend the standards of other women, she was primarily praised for conforming to ideals of feminine conduct. This illustrates the ambivalence of constructions of gender and their discursive discontinuities. Although her subjectivity was constructed in terms of gender difference, its ambivalence and representations of her individuality appeared to supersede such constructions. However, her individuality was only able to supersede the subject positions of others constructed as feminine, illustrating the power of patriarchal discourses of difference.

Kingsley was thus represented as both "womanly" and yet different from other women. For example, she was seen to possess "a wealth of adventurous experience which belongs to few men, and to no other woman, of this generation";[106] it was perceived that "in her travels she went through experiences that make one realise the courage and undaunted pluck a woman can exhibit";[107] while traveling, "she was quite ignorant of physical fear, a rather rare characteristic among women";[108] and, finally, her death was seen as

> a loss to science, to the literature of travel, and, above all, to the West African colonies, upon whose condition and administrative requirements she wrote with an authority possessed by few Englishmen, and certainly by no other Englishwoman.[109]

In all of these examples, Kingsley was seen as different from other women because of her travels, whereby she moved spatially and socially beyond the domestic constraints of Victorian patriarchy. Because her social transgressions were spatially distant and only possible when traveling away from "home," domestic constructions of the inferiority of women could remain unthreatened. Indeed, in several articles, Kingsley was praised as "a womanly woman."[110] The most extreme reference to Kingsley as superior to other women stated,

> Thousands of women could have better been spared of purposeless lives. It is a stirring and touching story of a life of self-sacrifice which nurtured no hope of recompensating glory in a vision of the martyr's crown.[111]

In contrast to the spatial displacement of constructions of gender difference and Kingsley's superiority acquired through traveling, other obituaries praised her exceptional femininity, as she transcended other women by conforming to rather than potentially challenging ideals of feminine conduct. For example, the obituary in the *Morning Leader* was entitled "Mary Kingsley: Her Charms as a Woman, Nurse, Cook, and Conversationalist Told by One Who Knew Her" and denied the importance of her identity as a traveler:

> Mary Kingsley the woman will hold a much more important place than Mary Kingsley the traveller. Women travellers we have enough and to spare; girls in Greenland, lasses at Lhassa, women wherever and whenever they are not wanted, and Mary Kingsley only differed from the rank and file of such in being able to write a clever book about her travels. Mary Kingsley the woman was a much rarer character whose keynote was unselfish devotion to duty—not imaginary duty far afield, but the duty which lay nearest her hand, and which was most plainly her own, and so long as any such duty remained to claim her energies she disregarded all her own wishes and interests.[112]

Even when her achievements were not explicitly attributed to her travels, Kingsley was still described as able to reconcile masculine and feminine behavior:

> Her high sense of duty and her love of truth, with her delicious humour, her capacity for hard work, and her unselfishness, followed her throughout her short span. . . . In her, masculine courage and intellect met feminine heart, devotion, and true simplicity.[113]

Kingsley's feminine attributes were also celebrated by Alice Stopford Green, who described her as "a skilled nurse, a good cook, a fine needlewoman, an accomplished housewife" and stated that it was her special gifts as a woman that gave to her work its unique and original character: in them lay her strength and her authority. She thought it may be truly said, through her heart: and it was in good measure the maternal instinct of protection and helpfulness that vivified her intelligence.[114]

The most vivid portrayals of Kingsley as feminine were descriptions of her appearance. These distinguished her from other women, countered preconceptions of her masculinity, and reproduced constructions of ideal feminine virtues. Most importantly, such descriptions often characterized her personality as inseparable from her appearance, making her the object of a masculine gaze rather than a subject in her own right. Descriptions of her appearance were often detailed, as shown by the following account:

> Rather under the medium height, slight, and somewhat spare, Mary Kingsley was fair in complexion and colouring. Her beautiful deep blue eyes were the most attractive feature in her face. . . . Always neatly and unobtrusively dressed, her fair hair was smoothly parted and arranged without trace of a fringe. She was fond of wearing an astrachan cap, which she pulled down firmly over her forehead. She traveled in ordinary costume, and found no use in "rational" clothes.[115]

Kingsley's appearance was not described as conventionally beautiful but was praised for its femininity, which differed from preconceptions of an intrepid, masculine traveler, illustrating the ambivalence of perceptions of her gendered subjectivity while traveling but the assertion of her femininity on her return. For example, Frank Bullen wrote that on their first meeting,

> I turned, expecting to see a masculine creature with a harsh voice and an air of command. Instead I saw a graceful, willowy figure, most womanly, the large eyes alight with vivacious expression and yet with something beseeching in them. A woman manifestly nervous . . .[116]

In contrast, and at times in direct contradiction, the *Manchester News* described Kingsley in a way that transcended conventional distinctions between masculinity and femininity:

> Miss Kingsley was tall, angular, but apparently of powerful physique. Her voice was somewhat strong, and her complexion darkened by tropical suns. She was moreover absolutely devoid of "nerves." But

although strong-minded and strong-bodied, hardened by rough travel, she lacked nothing of the refinement of the English gentlewoman.[117]

The ambivalence of constructions of gender difference can be seen in the paradoxical ways in which Kingsley's appearance reproduced ideals of feminine appearance while undermining ideals of feminine conduct. This paradox was resolved by displacing the latter to her travels while locating the former in the domestic sphere of "home." The distinction between "home" and away was textually reproduced by the contrasts arising from juxtaposing appropriate appearance with inappropriate conduct. For example, a correspondent in the *Highland News* described a visit to Kingsley:

> As she stood there in her drawing-room in a very feminine, even fashionable dress of soft grey, it was curiously difficult to realise her for what she was—a daring pioneer into the death-haunted unknown.[118]

Finally, in a similar way, E. D. Morel described Kingsley as a

> medium-sized, frail-looking woman, with the kindly face and smooth greyish hair, [who] you knew, had faced cannibal tribes, amongst whom the most experienced official or trader would not venture, if at all, without an armed escort.[119]

CONCLUSION

Kingsley was primarily perceived in terms of gendered identity on her return "home" in contrast to the imperial power and authority she shared through her racial identity while traveling. However, her gendered subjectivity and her mediation of public and private spheres were more ambivalent than fixed. This ambivalence can be extended to the differences perceived to exist between constructions of "home" and away. Kingsley's reception as a traveler, a writer, and a political figure was underlain by her marginal subject positionality as a woman. This marginality was itself inseparable from the tensions between the displacement achieved through traveling away from the context of Victorian patriarchy and the domestication arising from her return to it. Kingsley's correspondence illustrates how these tensions could arise from the coexistence of her public and private sense of duty both to Liverpool traders and to her family and friends.

As well as her personal presentations of public and private spheres, public recognition of Kingsley also reproduced the complex ambivalence of her subjectivity on her return. Representations of Kingsley changed over time, with reviews of *Travels in West Africa* emphasizing her character as traveler and author while reviews of *West African Studies* focused more on form, style, and content. The many published obituaries of Kingsley returned to a focus on her individuality, most graphically representing her as a gendered subject in terms of behavior and appearance. Such representations were, however, ambivalent because Kingsley was seen as surprisingly feminine, often more so than other women, while at the same time able to participate in roles perceived as masculine. This paradox can be resolved because her behavior was seen as both spatially and temporally differentiated with potentially masculine traits distanced in time and space from the celebration of her femininity on her return and current activities at "home." In this way, although Kingsley could be praised as superior to other women, this conceptualization did not challenge patriarchal constructions of women's subordination because it was located away from "home." Overall, the complex ambivalence of constructions of gendered subjectivity illustrate the reflexive relationship between the arbitrary and retrospective constructions of "home" and away and the distinctive representations of a woman who traveled between them.

NOTES

1. G. Van den Abbeele, *Travel as Metaphor: From Montaigne to Rousseau* (Minneapolis: University of Minnesota Press, 1992), as discussed in Chapter 1.

2. M. H. Kingsley, *Travels in West Africa: Congo, Français, Corsico and Cameroons* (London: Macmillan, 1897), 76.

3. Ibid., 506.

4. Ibid., 399.

5. *Times* December 2, 1895. This relates to Du Chaillu's travels in West Africa in the 1850s. He claimed to be the first white man to see a live gorilla, but this and other claims were so popular and sensationalist that he fell into disrepute among naturalists. It was not until the 1920s

that accounts were published that confirmed his claims. See R. West, *Brazza of the Congo—European Exploration and Exploitation in French Equatorial Africa* (London: Jonathan Cape, 1972).

Kingsley's publications were widely reviewed, but the *Times* was conspicuously silent. Kingsley stated, "I hate all newspapers" in a letter to John Holt of November 27, 1897, but she was most critical of the *Times*, which she described as "like the English government or the egg the poor curate got for breakfast when staying with his Bishop—parts of it are quite excellent—but it is in the main written by people who have been and who are in the Diplomatic Service. . . . Like the diplomatic service the Times knows nothing about West Africa, but it would *die* rather than own it" (Mary Kingsley to John Holt, February 21, 1898). The colonial editor at this time was Flora Shaw, and her relationship with Kingsley was perceived as distant and cool. In her correspondence with John Holt, Kingsley stated as early as December 2, 1897, "She won't know me and I don't want her to—*women!*" and later described her on February 20, 1899, as "a fine, handsome, bright upstanding young woman as clever as they make them, capable of an immense amount of hard work, as hard as nails, and talking like a 'Times' leader all the time. She refers to the Times as we, and does not speak of herself as a separate personality and leads you to think the Times is not a separate personality either." The perceived animosity between Kingsley and Flora Shaw seems to have been exaggerated; for example, Kingsley wrote to John Holt on January 21, 1899, concerning reviews of *West African Studies* that "the Times has not said one word. The gossip is that the Times means to wreak its most awful curse on me, not notice the book at all. It is said this action is inaugurated by Miss Flora Shaw who is commonly up here supposed to hate me, but I don't believe it, for I don't see why she would do so. I never interfere with her, and personally do not know her, but the Times is human inside, and I have been very uncivil to it—so I deserve all it can give." See H. Callaway and D. O. Helly, "Crusader for Empire: Flora Shaw/Lady Lugard," in *Western Women and Imperialism: Complicity and Resistance*, ed. N. Chaudhuri and M. Strobel (Bloomington: Indiana University Press,1992) for further discussion.

6. *Daily Telegraph*, December, 3, 1895.

7. Ibid.

8. Ibid.

9. Ibid., December 5, 1895.

10. J. P. Tompkins, "An Introduction to Reader-Response Criticism," in *Reader-Response Criticism: From Formalism to Post-structuralism*, ed. J. P. Tompkins (Baltimore: Johns Hopkins University Press, 1980).

11. Ibid.

12. As discussed in Chapter 2.

13. *Scottish Geographical Magazine* 13, 4 (April 1897): 215–217.

14. *New York Times*, February 13, 1897.

15. *Illustrated London News*, February 6, 1897.

16. *Morning Post*, January 14, 1897.

17. Ibid., January 21, 1897.

18. *Geographical Journal*, March 9, 1897, p. 324.

19. *West African News and Mining Review*, March 27, 1901.

20. *Leeds Mercury*, January 31, 1899.

21. *New York Times*, February 25, 1899.

22. *Daily Telegraph*, January 31, 1899.

23. *Spectator*, February 4, 1899. A further reference to Kingsley's place within a broader tradition of travel writing appeared in the *Western Daily Press*, January 31, 1899: "It seems to have passed into a recognized thing that everyone who goes far afield, or who finds his, or her, way into a comparatively unfrequented country, should call upon those who have been left at home to digest an account of the wanderers' impressions and experiences. But those who possess the gift of making a travel-book really interesting are comparatively few, so that works from the pens of established writers and travellers are always welcome."

24. *Daily Graphic*, January 31, 1899.

25. *Glasgow Herald*, January 31, 1899.

26. *Nottingham Daily Guardian*, January 31, 1899.

27. *Standard*, February 1, 1899.

28. *South Africa*, February 4, 1899.

29. *St. James Gazette*, January 31, 1899.

30. *Manchester Guardian*, January 31, 1899. In addition the *Sun* of February 3, 1899 stated, "One can feel how earnestly and conscientiously Miss Kingsley approaches her subject, setting forth her facts fearlessly, but drawing deductions with cautious reserve."

31. *Daily News*, January 31, 1899.

32. *Standard*, February 1, 1899.

33. *Glasgow Herald*, January 31, 1899.

34. *Echo*, January 31, 1899.

35. *Yorkshire Post*, February 1, 1899.

36. *New York Times*, June 5, 1897.

37. Mary Kingsley to Alice Stopford Green, undated (a). As summarized in D. Birkett, *Mary Kingsley—Imperial Adventures* (London: Macmillan, 1992), xx, Alice Stopford Green was from an established Anglo-Irish family and introduced Kingsley to many influential people. She organized the African Society after Kingsley's death.

38. Mary Kingsley to John Holt, January 21, 1898.

39. Mary Kingsley to John Holt, November 27, 1897.

40. Mary Kingsley to John Holt, April 29, 1898. In addition, Kingsley wrote to Alice Stopford Green on September 22, 1897 that "I am sick, dead sick, of people from which you will judge I have been doing my Society duty and seeing them."

41. Mary Kingsley to John Holt, February 21, 1898.

43. Mary Kingsley to Lady MacDonald, undated.

43. Mary Kingsley to Alice Stopford Green, September 28, 1897.

44. Mary Kingsley to Mrs. Gwynn, June 3, 1899.

45. D. Birkett, "An Independent Woman in West Africa: The Case of Mary Kingsley" (Ph.D. thesis, University of London, 1987), 202.

46. Mary Kingsley to John Holt, December 13, 1898.

47. Mary Kingsley to John Holt, April 25, 1899.

48. Mary Kingsley to John Holt, February 20, 1899. She wrote, "You do not know, Sir, how grateful I am to you for your toleration, how grateful I am to you for listening to me, like you would listen to a maiden aunt who tells you not to waste your money foolishly, not to be led away by grand talking people who give themselves airs. . . . Being a Kingsley I do hate humbug, and I do enjoy squashing it just as a maiden aunt objects to earwigs or 'Irish drapery.'"

49. Mary Kingsley to John Holt, March 9, 1899.

50. Mary Kingsley to Lord Cromer, September 25, 1899.

51. Mary Kingsley to Joseph Chamberlain, April 18, 1898.

52. Letter from Mary Kingsley published in the *Spectator*, March 19, 1898.

53. Birkett 1987. Birkett also notes that Mary Kingsley's letter was the first substantial article on the hut tax to appear in Britain. See Birkett 1992, and K. Frank, *A Voyager Out: The Life of Mary Kingsley* (Boston: Houghton Mifflin, 1986a), for further detail about Kingsley's political opinions and activities.

54. Mary Kingsley to E. D. Morel, February 20, 1899.

55. Letter from Mary Kingsley published in the *Spectator*, January 13, 1900.

56. Ibid.

57. Ibid.

58. Mary Kingsley to E. D. Morel, February 10, 1899.

59. Mary Kingsley to Joseph Chamberlain, September 3, 1899.

60. Mary Kingsley to Alice Stopford Green, undated, from RMS *Moor*, the Bay of Biscay. This was written in the context of the latter's involvement in Irish politics.

61. Mary Kingsley to Mrs. Holt, March 14, 1897. Kingsley continued to correspond with Mrs. Holt, largely referring to the state of her mental and physical health, and, in an undated letter, writing that she was aware that she was a trial for John Holt and that she relied on Mrs. Holt to ensure he did not worry "about my communications."

62. Mary Kingsley to Mrs. Holt, May 9, 1899.

63. Mary Kingsley to John Holt, May 5, 1898.

64. Mary Kingsley to John Holt, March 13, 1898.

65. Mary Kingsley to John Holt, March 19, 1898. My emphasis on the last sentence. John Holt obeyed these instructions, and his letter was published in the *Spectator* on March 26, 1898. He defended Kingsley's experience in West Africa and stated, "That lady has, I believe, a real liking for her negro friends. She will not allow them to be abused as sodden drunkards on the one hand, or on the other considered simply as machines to be utilised solely for the financial benefit of the European Government

which has taken possession of their country, without raising her voice in defence of both his character and his rights." The editor criticized this letter, stating that "our correspondent goes much too far in his generalizations. From challenging the expediency of a particular tax, as did Miss Kingsley, he slips into a general attack on our position." In a letter to John Holt written on March 27, 1898, Kingsley dismissed this criticism because "what old Townsend chooses to stick in as a note to it don't matter for it is *only* Townsend, not his readers" and stated that "Townsend *hates* blacks."

66. Mary Kingsley to E. D. Morel, February 20, 1899.

67. Mary Kingsley to E. D. Morel, March 22, 1899.

68. K. D. Nworah, "The Liverpool 'Sect' and British West African Policy 1895-1915," *African Affairs* 70, 281 (October 1971): 349-365; p. 350.

69. Ibid., 368.

70. Mary Kingsley to Alice Stopford Green, June 22, 1898.

71. Mary Kingsley to Hartland, March 16, 1897.

72. Mary Kingsley to Hartland, March 25, 1897.

73. Mary Kingsley to Christy, undated.

74. Letter from J. Arthur Hutton in *West Africa*, July 1900, 96.

75. Report of lecture at the Highgate Literary and Scientific Institute. The lecture was dated as March 23, 1897.

76. M. H. Kingsley, "A Lecture on West Africa," *Cheltenham Ladies College Magazine* 38 (Autumn 1898), 270.

77. Ibid., 280.

78. Reports of other lectures by Kingsley include "Travels on the Western Coast of Equatorial Africa," *Scottish Geographical Magazine* 12, 3 (March 1896): 113-124; *Times*, January 31, 1899, and February 14, 1900 (both accounts of lectures given at the Imperial Institute); "The Fetish View of the Human Soul," Folklore 8, 2 (June 1897): 138-151; and, finally, the report of the 714th Meeting of the Magpie and Stump Society in Cambridge (undated) at which "a very large majority" passed a motion proposed by Kingsley "that it is better for us to understand Alien Races than for Alien Races to understand us."

79. Mary Kingsley to George Macmillan, October 22, 1896.

80. Mary Kingsley to Dr. Günther, February 26, 1896.

81. Mary Kingsley to Lady MacDonald, undated (a).

82. Mary Kingsley to Dennis Kemp, undated (a).

83. Mary Kingsley to Mrs. Frazer, December 23, 1899.

84. Mary Kingsley to Mrs. Holt, January 1, 1899.

85. Mary Kingsley to Mrs. Holt, January 30, 1899.

86. Mary Kingsley to Dennis Kemp, undated (b), possibly May 1898.

87. Ibid.

88. Mary Kingsley to Sir Alfred Lyall, May 22, 1898.

89. Mary Kingsley to Alice Stopford Green, January 31, 1898.

90. Ibid.

91. Mary Kingsley to Lady MacDonald, undated (a).

92. Mary Kingsley to John Holt, January 29, 1898.

93. Mary Kingsley to John Holt, September 5, 1899. In addition to these two references, in her correspondence with Holt, Kingsley described her tiredness, depression, and illnesses in letters dated January 23, 1898; February 16, 1898; March 3, 1898; July 13, 1898; August 5, 1898; October 27, 1898; January 7, 1899; January 19, 1899; February 13, 1899; August 3, 1899; August 28, 1899; and September 30, 1899. The pattern of ill health at home compared with good—or at least unmentioned—health while traveling can be traced in a number of other women travelers. This can be interpreted as reflecting the medicalization of women in the context of Victorian domesticity, which could only be escaped by the independence gained through travel.

94. Mary Kingsley to Alice Stopford Green, April 11, 1900.

95. Ibid. As described by Birkett 1992, xx, John St. Loe Strachey was editor of the *Spectator* from 1898 and encouraged Kingsley's articles and letters.

96. Frank 1986a.

97. *Saturday Review*, June 9, 1900, 702.

98. *Times*, June 6, 1900.

99. *Athenaeum*, June 16, 1900, 750–751.

100. *Spectator*, June 16, 1900, 836. My emphasis.

101. *British Empire Review*, July 1900, 15.

102. Ibid.

103. For a discussion of the ideological significance of popular perceptions of Florence Nightingale, see M. Poovey, *Uneven Developments: The Ideological Work of Gender in Mid-Victorian England* (Chicago: University of Chicago Press, 1988).

104. *Topical Times*, June 16, 1900, 4. This continues: "I feel I must repeat of her, as Longfellow said of Florence Nightingale, with but one word altered: A lady with a Book shall stand, / In the great history of the land, / A noble type of good, / Heroic womanhood."

105. *Lady*, June 21, 1900, 976.

106. *Spectator*, June 16, 1900, 836.

107. *Western Mail*, June 23, 1900, 1, of the *Ladies' Supplement.*

108. Letter from Lewis Lusk in *Spectator*, June 23, 1900, 875–876.

109. *Manchester News*, June 9, 1900. In addition, the *Westminster Gazette* of June 6, 1900, stated that "her adventurous, lonely journeys in Africa, where Africa is deadliest and loneliest and most marvellous, had given Miss Kingsley a discipline which made her appear perfectly calm and collected under any circumstances."

110. In, for example, the *Western Mail*, June 23, 1900, 1, of the *Ladies Supplement* and *West Africa*, June 1900, 49.

111. E. Clodd, *Memories* (London: Chapman and Hall, 1916). Chapter 7 is entitled "Mary Henrietta Kingsley."

112. *Morning Leader*, June 14, 1900.

113. *Athenaeum* 3791, June 23, 1900, 784–785. This is echoed in *Mainly about People*, June 16, 1900, 670, in which Frank Bullen wrote that Kingsley was "a tender woman who coupled with her tenderness all the courage, energy, and will-power of the strongest man."

114. *Journal of the African Society* 1 (October 1901), 3.

115. *Pall Mall Gazette*, June 6, 1900, 3. This commentary is similar to an account in *Outlook*, June 9, 1900, which stated that "in Miss Kingsley's personal appearance there was little beyond the bright twinkling eyes, intelligent forehead, and alert manner to suggest the clever author and distinguished traveller. She used to be seen in a little black bonnet of by no means the newest shape, and even in wading the streams and pushing through the bush of West Africa she refused to compromise in the direction of abandoning skirts."

116. *Mainly about People*, June 16, 1900, 670. Frank Bullen went on to reiterate his "surprise at the difference between the Mary Kingsley I had imagined and this sweet-voiced, most feminine reality."

117. *Manchester News*, June 9, 1900.

118. *Highland News*, June 16, 1900, 12. This obituary of Kingsley was printed in the column "For the Ladies."

119. *West Africa*, June 1900, 51.

Institutional Responses to Women Travel Writers

As well as the reviews, articles, and obituaries published about Mary Kingsley and her writings, broader institutional parameters informed the reconstitution of "home" for women travel writers on their return. In this chapter I focus on two examples, namely, the debates concerning the admission of women as fellows of the RGS;[1] and attempts to identify Kingsley and other women travel writers of the 1890s as "new women." Although such debates were often tangential and at times in direct opposition to Kingsley's interests, they were significant in influencing the public climate of opinion and reception of women travel writers more generally.

THE ROYAL GEOGRAPHICAL SOCIETY AND WOMEN FELLOWS

Kingsley was vehemently opposed to women's suffrage and to the admission of women to societies such as the RGS, arguing in the latter case that

> if we women distinguish ourselves in Science in sufficiently large numbers at a sufficiently high level the great Scientific Societies . . . will admit women on their own initiative or we shall form Scientific Societies of our own of equal eminence.[2]

However, in the same letter, she became self-effacing, stating that

I have no right to speak at all. . . . In science I am only a collector of specimens and as a traveller, though I have travelled further in West Africa than any of my countrymen still I have never fixed a point or taken an observation or in fact done any surveying work that entitles me to be called a geographer.[3]

Kingsley expanded on her opinions in her next letter to John Scott Keltie. She believed that the presence of women would inhibit scientific discussion both because of the need for propriety and because of the interests of women themselves. In the former case, she wrote that if women were admitted to large scientific societies such as the RGS, "I sincerely hope . . . they will make a separate Department—or let the ladies have a separate council Chamber in which they can speak their minds."[4] Kingsley illustrated her claim by referring to the Anthropological Institute,[5] stating that

the presence of ladies is hindersome to the gentlemen. It is not hindersome to me because I can go and tell Tylor or in extreme cases Mrs Tylor, who can tell him why they kill twins in West Africa and such like things.[6]

In this way Kingsley perceived herself as separate from both women and men in scientific societies and revealed the importance of private channels of communication, often through a female contact. In the latter case—how the interests of women would lower the scientific standards of the RGS—Kingsley wrote that

your terms for admitting men are too low to stand it. Then the tone would fall to the level of the main body of the ladies['] interests—sensational adventures etc would take the place of your truly geographical papers on sub-oceanic changes and the geography of mammals etc.[7]

Again, Kingsley detached herself from other women and echoed arguments expressed within the RGS in opposition to the admission of women as fellows.

The debates concerning the admission of women as fellows of the RGS potentially threatened the masculinity that seemed to inform its imperialist role. This was most graphically conveyed by the anniversary address of 1887, in which the president stated,

What we require . . . is precise and accurate information of the earth's surface, however it may be obtained, and to train the minds of our youth in the powers of observation sufficient to enable them to obtain this information; if in so doing our countrymen continue to be stimulated to deeds of daring, to enterprise and adventures, to self-denial and hardships, it will assist in preserving the manhood of our country, which is more and more endangered year by year in consequence of our endeavour to keep peace within our own borders and to stave off strife with our neighbours.[8]

Despite their ineligibility for fellowship, two women received awards from the RGS in the 1860s. Lady Franklin received the Founder's Gold Medal in 1860 for her "devotion" in financing expeditions searching for her husband who died in the discovery of the Northwest Passage.[9] In 1869 Mary Somerville received the Victoria Medal, but her feminine attributes were similarly seen as equally if not more important than her contributions to geographical knowledge, the *Journal of the RGS* praising her because

in addition to her researches into the phenomena of the heavens and the earth, [she] has also excelled in the arts of painting, music and all feminine accomplishments.[10]

However, it was not until the 1890s that debates concerning women fellows reached their height. In July 1892 the council unanimously decided to admit women as fellows, and in November the first 15 were elected to a fellowship of over 3,000.[11] A small group of fellows, most with naval or military titles, organized opposition to the women's admission and proposed a motion that was discussed at a special general meeting in April 1893, by which time a total of 21 women had been elected. A motion in favor of admitting women was defeated by 147 votes to 105. But debate continued, seven letters on the subject were printed in the *Times*, and a circular vote was held, with 1,165 in favor, 100 agreeing to their admission under various restrictions, and 465 opposed to women fellows. Another special general meeting was held in July 1893, and despite the result of the circular vote, a motion to admit women fellows was defeated, with 158 in favor and 172 against. It was agreed that the women already elected could remain fellows but that no more would be elected, and this remained the case until November 1912. At a referendum held in January 1913, the motion to admit women fellows was finally passed and accepted, 26 years after it was first proposed.

The main arguments in support of women fellows included the need for money to finance the relocation of the society; competition particularly from the Royal Scottish Geographical Society, which had admitted women since its foundation in 1884[12] and which had recently opened a regional branch in London; and, most immediately, the unwillingness of Isabella Bird Bishop[13] to write a paper to be read by a man because of her ineligibility to be elected a fellow. These essentially pragmatic concerns were inseparable from underlying constructions of gender difference. I focus here on the implications of such constructions for the representation of women travel writers in the private sphere of debate within the RGS itself, the public sphere of correspondence to the *Times*, and the legal sphere as both sides sought advice that changed the terms, form, and content of the debate. I address not only the content of the debates but also the form and language through which they were articulated.

Support for women fellows was most strongly expressed in an anonymous letter to the *Times* published in May 1893; it asked,

> Will it be alleged by any serious or sensible person that Mrs Bishop is not a better Fellow, a better traveller, a better writer, and a more thorough Geographer than 19-20ths of the 3500 male Fellows? Can it be argued that an average woman is not as useful as a member of the Society as an average schoolmaster, or clergyman, or retired officer?[14]

At a meeting of the RGS, the differences between the explorations of men and women were identified when one fellow posed the following question:

> The Society has frequently given sums ranging from one hundred to five thousand pounds towards geographical exploration and you have honoured your travellers who have come back, why not honour the ladies who pay their own way and bring to you the results of their explorations and discoveries.[15]

Corresponding to the concerns of "new geography," it was also argued that the RGS was playing an increasingly important role in education and that it was shortsighted to exclude women teachers from its fellowship. However, this argument was used by those

opposed to the admission of women fellows because they believed
it would lower the class status of the RGS, with one fellow remarking, "I think the Society should not be a registry office for teachers
and governesses and that kind of thing."[16] It was argued that the
admission of women would lower the scientific as well as class
credentials of the RGS, an opinion most forcibly expressed in a letter
to the *Times* from George Curzon in May 1893:

> We contest *in toto* the general capability of women to contribute to
> scientific geographical knowledge. Their sex and training render them
> equally unfitted for exploration; and the genus of professional female
> globetrotters with which America has lately familiarized us is one of
> the horrors of the latter end of the nineteenth century.[17]

In this letter the existence of women travelers was displaced away
from Britain so that as well as undermining the scientific and social
integrity of the RGS, the admission of women fellows would potentially threaten its national, imperialist strength. Such concerns were
also expressed in meetings of the RGS, with one fellow, for example, fearing that

> if we had ladies here as a matter of right it would be more the object
> of the Council to provide for their amusement than for the progress
> of Scientific Research, that we should have lectures at which the popu-
> lar element would predominate. We have already magic lanterns and
> dissolving views, in a short time we should probably have a piano.[18]

Despite such arguments, women had always been admitted to
lectures as guests, and, as Kingsley found, information was forthcoming for women who intended to travel.[19] It therefore seems that
the status of the RGS was seen as threatened by women only if they
became formal subscribers able to call themselves fellows. An
underlying theme was the value of the initials FRGS, with opposing fellows arguing that

> there is in the outside world, I am not saying our own eyes we know
> the value of F.R.G.S., which is practically nothing, but in the eyes
> of the outside world a somewhat real value given to these letters and
> the idea of [admitting women fellows] in so far as it is made on behalf
> of certificated teachers and mistresses of Board schools is in order
> that they may have a fictitious value put after their names.[20]

In other words, it was acknowledged within the RGS that being a fellow was virtually worthless, but that to those outside it had some market value that should be maintained and that would be undermined by the admission of women.

Despite these arguments, most of the debate within the society avoided the actual issues by focusing on constitutional legality. Freshfield, one of the honorary secretaries of the RGS, criticized the tactics of fellows opposing the admission of women as "a military and naval manoeuvre,"[21] and the hierarchy within the RGS was criticized because it seemed to threaten individual autonomy. One fellow used imagery similar to Freshfield's when he stated that

> in voting on the question of women or no women we are voting on the question of whether we govern ourselves or are to be governed by the real quarterdeck in this Society.[22]

Such an emphasis on fellows' rights—and how these had been violated by the council's mismanagement of the situation—was very class-specific. For example, in a letter to the *Times* in June 1893, Admiral M'Clintock argued that the council had not publicized its decision to admit women fellows widely enough; although a notice had appeared in the *Journal of the RGS*, this was "in the month of August, at a time therefore when everyone almost is away from London."[23]

Much attention focused on the issue of language. A fellow opposing the admission of women asked "Can you turn he into she? Can you turn Chairman into Chairmaness?"[24] Such arguments were supported by legal discourse that stated,

> The admission of Ladies was never contemplated at the time the Charter was granted which is proved by the fact that in the Rules of the Society the references to the Fellows are always made in the terms "he" "his" or "Gentlemen" and these terms occur in the rules thirty eight times.[25]

All proposals supporting the admission of women fellows were accompanied by an interpretation clause stating that all masculine pronouns would be seen to include women. In this way, even if women were admitted, the rules would not be changed; rather, women would be subsumed within a masculine discourse.

The debates concerning the admission of women to the RGS illustrate institutional mismanagement, the equation of gender difference with class status, and the desire to avoid the issues by highlighting constitutional procedure. It is ironic that the president of the society in 1913, when women were admitted, was George Curzon, who had written the letter to the *Times* most vehement in its opposition to the admission of women fellows in 1893.

"NEW WOMEN" OF THE 1890s

"New women" of the 1890s challenged gendered divisions of labor, the ideal of the bourgeois home, and a fixed class hierarchy.[26] According to Ann Ardis, the category "new woman" differed from the Victorian "angel in the house," single-issue social reformers, "independent women" who relied on their middle-class status to endorse themselves professionally, and middle-class women socialists who emphasized class rather than gender inequalities.[27] To be labeled, or to label oneself, a "new woman" had important social, economic, and political implications.

Women novelists of the 1890s were often described as "new women." The changing structure and organization of publishing in the 1890s provided more opportunities for women to be published, and this occurred to such an extent that

> the common perception in the 1890s was that women were taking over the literary world. New publishing houses, new audiences for fiction, new publication formats: all were seen to give women writers, particularly previously unpublished women writers, a distinct advantage in the literary marketplace.[28]

Descriptions of Kingsley as a "new woman" thus related not only to broad social, economic, and political imperatives but also to more specifically literary contexts. In this section I discuss the extent to which Kingsley was described as a "new woman" in the context of her identity as a traveler and/or writer, her opposition to this description, and how she was perceived as a model for other "new women" to emulate.

The *Daily Telegraph* referred to Kingsley as "a 'New Woman' of the nobler sort" but proceeded to state, "We should, indeed, be far from recommending solitary travel in Africa, or in similarly barbarous regions, to any woman—even to the New Woman."[29] Kingsley adamantly opposed this description of her; in a reply to this article, she wrote,

> I do not relish being called a New Woman. I am not one in any sense of the term. Every child I come across tyrannizes over me, and a great deal of time I ought to give to science goes in cooking, &c. I do not think travelling now lays one open to this reproach.[30]

Most references to Kingsley as a "new woman" were in obituaries published in women's journals. She was described as a model for other women, and this served as a vehicle for implicit and explicit criticism of "new women." For example,

> Mary Kingsley was one of the most wonderful women of her age, a lesson on the one hand to the indolent woman of the world ever seeking for fresh excitement to sting her out of langour, and, on the other, to the aggressive working woman who thinks work can't be done in skirts, and that it is "superior" to talk contemptuously of men.[31]

Kingsley was seen as different from other women because she was able to reconcile potentially masculine achievements with her essential femininity. It was argued that

> in these days, when so much is said about women's work, and an impression seems to prevail that in order to accomplish any kind of work it is necessary for women to wholly sink their sexship, it is refreshing to be able to point out one who contrived not only to achieve fame for herself, but to do infinite credit to her sex, and yet not to lose a jot or little of the charm of womanhood.[32]

Furthermore, in contrast to the external trademarks of "new women," "divided skirts and the 'indispensible' cigarette were not in her way."[33]

Kingsley's opinions of "new women" can be most clearly discerned in the political context of campaigns for women's suffrage.

On one occasion she expressed the belief that women's suffrage would only serve to "make our political machinery more cumbersome."[34] On another occasion she wrote to John Holt about her refusal to attend a "women's conference":

> They came down on me, four of them and no good looks to spare, to ask me why I had never given help or sympathy to the enfranchisement of women! I said because I thought it a very minor question. While there was a most vital section of Englishmen unenfranchised women could wait. . . . I explained that men would always be chivalrous to women and strive to protect their best interests, that every voting Englishman was a representative of women, but he wasn't of men of another class to his own.[35]

In another letter to John Holt, she scornfully described such women as "shrieking females, and androgens."[36] Kingsley perceived not only race and gender but also class and gender as essential and distinct categories. In this way, she perceived West Coast traders to belong to a lower class from those with power and influence in government, and her desire to see traders rather than women enfranchised reflected her desire for their political influence and credibility in imperial policymaking. This position is most clearly articulated in a further letter to John Holt, in which she forcefully stated,

> A vote in the conduct of the affairs of the British Empire you have *not* got, and you *are* a citizen of the Empire, representing one of England's most important interests, but unrepresented politically. I suppose so far as the commercial men in England are as a body prosperous and busy they will be content with their ladylike position, but I think it would be well if they insisted on having the full vote.[37]

Kingsley explicitly correlates a lack of power with femininity, but rather than perceive the need for structural change in gender relations, she portrays traders as victims of political inequality.

It may seem paradoxical that Kingsley—who was able to gain independence only by traveling beyond the domestic responsibilities of "home"—was opposed to women's suffrage. This suggests the tensions of mediating "home" and away, private and public spheres, all of which were underpinned by complex and ambivalent constructions of difference. Such a paradox thus clearly reflects the spatial as well as social parameters of traveling. Women such as Kingsley often traveled for personal reasons linked to a desire to escape the confinement of domesticity. However, their travels and travel writing often caused them to enter the public sphere, where it was necessary to legitimize their motives in terms of scientific and professional interests. This tension reflects the tension between femininity and the traits of masculinity while traveling. The desire to be distanced from suffragists and "new women" could thus stem from the need for women travel writers to legitimize their travels and writings in the masculine, public realm of scientific research, professionalism, and politics that arose from their construction as feminine on their return "home."

CONCLUSION

The debates concerning the admission of women as fellows to the RGS and the literary and political constructions of "new women" in the 1890s represent two broader contexts within which to situate women travel writers on their return "home." Although many of the debates were tangential to Kingsley's travels and writings, they were important in informing attitudes toward her. Kingsley's opposition to women's becoming fellows of the RGS and to women's suffrage illustrates her ambivalent subject positionality as she moved within and between the spheres of "home" and away, private and public, both on her travels and on her return.

NOTES

1. See the Introduction for more on the RGS, "new imperialism," and "new geography" of the late nineteenth century. According to the *Proceedings of the RGS and Monthly Record of Geography* N.S. 9 (1887), "The privileges of a Fellow include admission (with one friend) to all meetings of the Society, and the use of the library and Map room. Each Fellow is also entitled to receive a copy of the New Monthly Series of the Proceedings and the Supplementary Papers."
2. Mary Kingsley to Mrs. Farquharson, November 26, 1899. Kingsley was replying to Mrs. Farquharson's request that she support a petition for the admission of women to the RGS. Kingsley enclosed a copy of her letter to John Scott Keltie, honorary secretary of the RGS, on November 27, 1899, and wrote to him that "I do not wish to alarm you but I feel it is my

duty as a friend to warn you that there is a dangerous female after you, I enclose details. I'm terrified of her."

3. Mary Kingsley to Mrs. Farquharson, November 26, 1899.

4. Mary Kingsley to John Scott Keltie, December 1, 1899.

5. The Anthropological Society of London was formed by twelve fellows leaving the Ethnological Society of London in 1863. One of the reasons for this split was over the admission of women. The Ethnological Society—unlike the Anthropological Society—was in favor of admitting women. The two societies were reunited to form the Anthropological Institute in 1871, but women were not admitted as members until 1876. See V. Careless, "The Ethnological Society of London, 1843-1871" (M.A. thesis, University of British Columbia, 1974).

6. Mary Kingsley to John Scott Keltie, December 1, 1899.

7. Ibid.

8. The "Annual Address on the Progress of Geography, 1886-1887," delivered by General R. Strachey at the anniversary meeting, May 23, 1887, in *Proceedings of the RGS and Monthly Record of Geography* N.S. 9 (1887), 630.

9. *Journal of the RGS* 30 (1860).

10. Ibid., 39 (1869), cxxxiii.

11. See the appendix to this volume for a list of the original women fellows. All references for the following discussion are from the "Ladies Box" of RGS Additional Papers 93-99.

12. D. Birkett, "An independent woman in West Africa: The case of Mary Kingsley" (Ph.D. thesis, University of London, 1987). As noted in the Introduction, the Manchester, Newcastle, and Liverpool geography societies all admitted women. Other societies that admitted women at their foundation included the Royal Entomological Society (founded 1833), the Royal Botanical Society (1839), the Geologists Association (1858), the Imperial Institute (1888), and the British Empire League (1899). The Royal Society (founded 1662) admitted women in 1945, the Linnaean Society (1788) in 1904, the Geological Society (1807) in 1919, the Royal Asiatic Society (1823) in 1856, the British Association (1831) in 1843, and the Royal Colonial Institute (1868) in 1922. All from Birkett 1987, 341. The African Society—founded in 1901 in memory of Mary Kingsley—admitted women from the time of its foundation.

13. Isabella Bird Bishop (1831-1904) traveled, most notably, across the Rocky Mountains, India, Persia, Korea, China, and Japan, largely on horseback, and wrote nine books about her travels. See P. Barr, *A Curious Life for a Lady: The Story of Isabella Bird, Traveller Extraordinary* (London: Penguin, 1986).

14. Letter to the *Times* from "A Bona Fide Traveler," May 29, 1893.

15. Report of the special general meeting, November 28, 1892.

16. Ibid., April 24, 1893.

17. Letter from George N. Curzon to the *Times*, May 31, 1893.

18. Report of the special general meeting, April 24, 1893.

19. This is evident in Kingsley's correspondence with John Scott Keltie. For example, she thanked him for the RGS *Hints to Travellers* on December 14, 1895; she thanked him for a copy of the *Journal* on January 5, 1896; she sent notes requesting information on March 28, 1896, and April 1, 1896; and on January 13, 1897, she wrote that "I have often wished to call and ask you things, but they were matters of small importance and I feared you might think me encroaching."

20. Report of the special general meeting, April 24, 1893.

21. Ibid.

22. Ibid.

23. Letter from Admiral F. Leopold M'Clintock to the *Times*, June 1, 1893.

24. Report of the special general meeting, April 24, 1893.

25. Letter from R. Webster and H. Sutton proposing a joint case to be submitted to counsel, December 10, 1892.

26. A. L. Ardis, *New Women, New Novels: Feminism and Early Modernism* (New Brunswick, NJ: Rutgers University Press, 1990).

27. Ibid.

28. Ibid., 43.

29. *Daily Telegraph*, December 3, 1895.

30. Ibid., December 5, 1895.

31. *Lady*, June 21, 1900.

32. *Lady's Pictorial*, June 16, 1900.

33. Ibid.

34. Mary Kingsley to John Holt, undated (a).

35. Mary Kingsley to John Holt, July 11, 1899.

36. Mary Kingsley to John Holt, undated (a).

37. Mary Kingsley to John Holt, September 5, 1899.

CONCLUSION

A lady an explorer? A traveller in skirts?
The notion's just a trifle too seraphic.
Let them stay at home and mind the babies,
    or hem our ragged shirts;
But they mustn't, can't and shan't be geographic![1]

Despite the hopes of this verse of 1839, women in the nineteenth-century did travel and should be considered "geographic." Women travelers experienced new places, and women travel writers described such places to readers at home. The geographies of women's travels and writings were inseparable from their own and others' perceptions of their identity. Such perceptions also had their own geographies, varying over space as well as time as women mediated the spheres of "home" and away while traveling and writing about their travels.

Travel writing by women should not be studied in isolation from three underlying themes, namely, the significance of travel and travel writing; the distinctive nature of imperial representation; and how both travel writing and imperial representation were differentiated by constructions of gender. Ideologies of otherness should be destabilized to give voice to those marginalized by such totalizations. Colonizing as well as colonized women have been silenced by colonial discourse. Rather than replicate imperial strategies of totalization, a consideration of discourses of difference along lines of gender, race, and class reveals their ambivalence. I have focused on a woman travel writer to illuminate the spatial differentiation and textual representation of such discourses. By studying imperial women travel writers, patriarchal and imperial discursive formations can be seen to have shaped and constrained subjectivity over space and time as women traveled within and between the spheres of "home" and away.

"Departure" denoted constructions of gendered subjectivity both prior to and during a journey. I have related poststructuralist notions of the "death of the author" to constructions of author positionality, and illustrated this with reference to *Travels in West Africa*. In the context of preparations for departure, motives, expectations, conduct books, and general logistics were clearly differentiated by gender. In terms of gendered subjectivity while traveling, Mary Kingsley's textual representations of herself and others relate to broader issues of observation and ethnography. Overall, unstable and ambivalent constructions of gender difference informed and emerged from Kingsley's travels and writings.

Kingsley appears to have been primarily constructed in terms of gender subordination while at home but able, while on her travels, temporarily to share in racial superiority in the context of imperial power and authority. Such constructions were, however, ambivalent rather than fixed, as reflected by the textual polyphony of her travel writing. This ambivalence also extended to political spheres, with Kingsley publicly supporting imperialism but privately empathizing with Africans because of her split position as both inside and outside Western discourses of power and authority. Constructions of gender were similarly ambivalent over space, with Kingsley adopting both masculine and feminine voices and codes of conduct on her travels and in her writings. Kingsley's contradictory subject position is particularly evident in her landscape descriptions. Her subjective identification with places as well as people coexisted with attempts to emulate more masculine, imperial strategies of objectifying vision. Kingsley's empathy with West Coast traders reflected her desire to reconcile this tension because she believed that traders should influence policy because of their local knowledge of West Africa and Africans.

In contrast to her ability to share in imperial power and authority while traveling, Kingsley was primarily perceived in terms of gendered identity on her return "home." However, her gendered subjectivity and her mediation of both public and private spheres were more ambivalent than fixed, as were the differences perceived to exist between "home" and away. This was apparent in her own and others' representations of her travels and writings. It seems paradoxical that Kingsley was considered surprisingly feminine and even more feminine than other women despite—and yet because of—having participated in roles regarded as masculine. This can in part be resolved because her behavior was seen as spatially and temporally differentiated. Her potentially masculine traits were distanced in space and time, but her femininity was reasserted on her return "home." Although she was often described as superior to other women, this status did not challenge patriarchal constructions of women's subordination because it was displaced away from "home."

Imperial women's travels and their writings were clearly distinctive in material ways. These ranged from preparations prior to departure, the nature of the journey, and the reception of both women and their writings on their return. In this way, it seems clear that a journey itself represents only one moment of traveling, inseparable from departure and return. Because of the gendered significance of material travel, the metaphorical immanence of travel should also be seen as clearly gendered. Implications include the inseparability of discourses of power, "truth" and knowledge, and, more tangibly, the need to deconstruct theory, "home," and difference.

A theme that has emerged throughout my discussion has been the importance of public and private spheres of influence, relating to spatial and temporal differentiation within the contexts of "home" and away as well as while traveling between them. This can be traced at all stages of travel and travel writing. For example, women were defined primarily in the private, domestic sphere before traveling into more public spheres. On their return, these spheres often coexisted, with private and public recognition and responsibilities redefining "home." In terms of writing, women travelers often based their published accounts on private letters and diaries, and their public roles were often underpinned by private networks and channels for communication, as shown by Kingsley's prolific correspondence. Women travel writers celebrated their personal independence achieved through travel but often opposed more universal opportunities for independence, such as women's suffrage. This apparent paradox reflects the tensions of legitimating private fulfillment within the public context of political and professional parameters. The coexistence of public and private spheres and the ways in which women moved within and between them suggests that attempts to dichotomize them should be deconstructed.

A further concern relates to studying an individual without celebrating individuality. I have focused on the travels and writings of Kingsley to illustrate far-reaching themes. These include constructions of difference in the constitution and contestation of subjectivity; the ambivalence of imperial representations; the material and metaphorical significance of travel; and the potential offered by feminism and poststructuralism for writing histories, geographies, historical geographies, and historiographies. I have attempted to ground these themes in my study of Kingsley, whom I view as discursively positioned rather than biographically defined. Such a subject offers many opportunities for vivid description that is neither unique nor universal. Kingsley is not a closed subject for understanding; rather, the complex ambivalence of her subject positionality over space and time should facilitate multiple interpretations.

In the Introduction, I outlined three broad contexts for my study of women travel writers and imperialism, namely, the study of women in history, Western women and imperialism, and women and the history of geography. For all of these areas of study, I hope that my work on Kingsley has shown that a consideration of a subject depends on critical awareness of constructions of subjectivity. The substantive implications of studying a woman's travel writing and imperialism are inseparable from epistemological and methodological concerns. Poststructuralist, postcolonial, and feminist attempts to deconstruct the other by foregrounding difference often overlap in their desire to escape totalizing, imperial metanarratives. Such attempts often translate into a sense of heightened self-consciousness about one's own and others' representations. Writing itself, and particularly writing other people and places, has come under closer scrutiny, often involving a greater awareness of historical, academic, and institutional legacies. Imperial women travelers should not merely be added to histories of geography but should prompt questions about those histories themselves. Feminists who attempt to rectify the neglect of Western women and imperialism should be conscious that feminism itself emerged at a time of imperialism.[2] Finally, to incorporate women into historical study should serve to critique ethnocentric and patriarchal silencing. In all of these broad contexts, however, gender difference should be seen as inseparable from many other constructions of difference. Although it is often strategic to highlight one over others, such constructions are not essential in their differences. Their interactions should instead be traced through both space and time to expose the complex relationships among power, "truth," and knowledge.

The three interpretations of "Only a Woman" with which I began the Introduction are inextricably intertwined. Women's travel writing was distinctive in the ways that women traveled, how they wrote about their travels, and how both their travels and writings were received. Patriarchal constructions of gender difference were powerful forces promoting such distinctiveness. The neglect of women travel writers and women in imperialism more generally also reflects patriarchal constructions of gender difference. In this way, the more positive potential of "Only a Woman" relates to attempts to study women and the challenges that arise from such study. In looking at Kingsley, I have faced such challenges as coming to terms with her imperial politics and her opposition to women's suffrage and the admission of women to societies such as the RGS. Finally, "Only a Woman" relates to the significance of women traveling alone and the need to recognize their individual but often multiple identities without perpetuating stereotypes or celebrating heroism. In my study of Kingsley, a consideration of subject positionality has revealed the construction and contestation not only of subjectivity but also of space itself.

NOTES

1. This anonymous verse appeared in Punch in 1839 and is cited by D. Birkett, *Spinsters Abroad: Victorian Lady Explorers* (Oxford: Basil Blackwell, 1989).

2. See, for example, A. M. Burton, "The White Woman's Burden: British Feminists and the Indian Woman, 1865–1915," *Women's Studies International Forum* 13, 4 (1990): 295–308. This is reprinted in part in N. Chaudhuri and M. Strobel, eds., *Western Women and Imperialism: Complicity and Resistance* (Bloomington: Indiana University Press, 1992).

Primary Source Material

BOOKS BY MARY KINGSLEY

Kingsley, M. H. *Travels in West Africa: Congo Français, Corisco and Cameroons*. London: Macmillan, 1897. London: Virago, 1986.
Kingsley, M. H. *West African Studies*. London: Macmillan, 1899.
Kingsley, M. H. *The Story of West Africa*. London: Horace Marshall, 1900.

NEWSPAPERS AND JOURNALS

Articles and Reports of Lectures by Mary Kingsley

British Empire Review	August 1899
	October 1899
Cheltenham Ladies College Magazine	Autumn 1898
Imperial Institute Journal	March 1899
	April 1900
Mainly about People	May 20, 1899
Times	January 31, 1899
	February 14, 1900
West Africa and Traders Review	July 1900
Illustrated	February 1901

Letters from Mary Kingsley

Daily Telegraph	December 5, 1895
Saturday Review	February 18, 1899
	February 25, 1899
Spectator	December 28, 1895
	May 15, 1897
	March 19, 1898
	January 13, 1900

Reviews of Travels in West Africa

Geographical Journal	March 1897
Illustrated London News	February 6, 1897
Morning Post	January 14, 1897
	January 21, 1897
New York Times	February 13, 1897
	June 5, 1897
Spectator	March 6, 1897

Reviews of West African Studies

Daily Chronicle	January 25, 1899
Daily Graphic	January 31, 1899
Daily News	January 31, 1899
Daily Telegraph	January 31, 1899
Dundee Advertiser	January 31, 1899
Eastern Daily Press	January 31, 1899
Echo	January 31, 1899
Geographical Journal	April 1899
Glasgow Herald	January 31, 1899
Illustrated London News	March 11, 1899
Leeds Mercury	January 31, 1899
Manchester Guardian	January 31, 1899
Morning Post	January 31, 1899
New York Times	February 25, 1899
Nottingham Daily Guardian	January 31, 1899
St. James Gazette	January 31, 1899
Saturday Review	February 4, 1899
Scotsman	January 31, 1899
South Africa	February 4, 1899
Spectator	February 4, 1899
Standard	February 1, 1899
Sun	February 3, 1899

West African News and African Mining Review	March 27, 1901
Western Daily Press	January 31, 1899
Yorkshire Post	February 1, 1899

Obituaries of Mary Kingsley

British Empire Review	July 1900
The Churchwoman	June 15, 1900
The Gentlewoman	June 16, 1900
Geographical Journal	July 1900
Highland News	June 16, 1900
Illustrated London News	June 9, 1900
The Lady	June 21, 1900
Lady's Pictorial	June 16, 1900
New York Times	June 6, 1900
Pall Mall Gazette	June 6, 1900
	June 11, 1900
St. James Gazette	June 9, 1900
Saturday Review	June 9, 1900
Spectator	June 16, 1900
Standard	June 6, 1900
Times	June 6, 1900
Topical Times	June 16, 1900
Western Mail	June 23, 1900
Westminster Gazette	June 6, 1900

Other Articles and Letters about Mary Kingsley

British Empire Review	February 1900
Daily Chronicle	November 27, 1897
Daily Telegraph	December 3, 1899
Geographical Journal	January 1896
Illustrated London News	January 4, 1896
Journal of the African Society	1901–1902

London Review	May 21, 1898
New York Times	January 10, 1896
Saturday Review	February 18, 1899
Spectator	June 23, 1900
	November 23, 1901
Times	December 2, 1895
	June 7, 1900
	June 26, 1900
	August 7, 1900
	August 8, 1900
	August 14, 1900
	August 17, 1900
West Africa and Traders Review Illustrated	June 1900
	July 1900
	August 1900
	November 1900
	December 1900
	March 9, 1901
	June 1, 1901
	June 22, 1901
	June 29, 1901
	July 6, 1901
	July 13, 1901
	October 5, 1901
	October 19, 1901
	December 28, 1901
West African News and African Mining Review	March 6, 1901
	June 26, 1901

General Articles and Letters about West Africa

Saturday Review	February 11, 1899
	March 4, 1899
	March 11, 1899
Spectator	December 7, 1895
	March 26, 1898
West Africa and Traders Review Illustrated	September 14, 1901
	October 12, 1901

West African News and	February 27, 1901
African Mining Review	March 6, 1901
	March 27, 1901
	April 17, 1901
	May 8, 1901
	May 22, 1901
	June 12, 1901

Macmillan Correspondence

147 letters and fragments of letters from Mary Kingsley to George Macmillan, July 1893 to August 1899. (Source: 54914 Macmillan Archive, The British Library.)

5 letters from Henry Guillemard to Mary Kingsley; 1 letter from Mary Kingsley to Henry Guillemard. (Source: 54914 Macmillan Archive, the British Library.)

ROYAL GEOGRAPHICAL SOCIETY

Correspondence

4 letters from Mary Kingsley to Violet Paget Roy, 1893.

Correspondence from Mary Kingsley to John Scott Keltie, December 1895 to December 1899.

Correspondence from Isabella Bird Bishop to John Scott Keltie, October 1888 to August 1898.

"Ladies Box": RGS Additional Papers 93–99

Letters from August 1892 to March 1894 concerning the admission of women fellows.

Reports of special general meetings on November 28, 1892, April 24, 1893 and July 3, 1893.

Extracts from council minutes June 27, 1887 to July 4, 1892 and November 4, 1912.

Legal documents from December 1892 to April 1893 and November 1912.

Reports and Correspondence in the Times

| Report of Anniversary Dinner | May 15, 1893 |
| Letter from "A Bona Fide Traveller" | May 29, 1893 |

Report of Annual Meeting	May 30, 1893
Letter from G. Curzon	May 31, 1893
Letter from F. L. M'Clintock	June 1, 1893
Letter from W. H. Russell	June 1, 1893
Letter from D. W. Freshfield	June 3, 1893
Letter from G. Curzon	June 5, 1893
Letter from W. Hicks	June 10, 1893

Journals at the Royal Geographical Society

Journal of the RGS 30, 1860 p. xciv: Founder's Gold Medal to Lady Franklin; and 39, 1869 p. cxxxiii: Patron's or Victoria Medal to Mrs. Mary Somerville.

Geographical Journal, June 1897, pp. 589–604: Report of Anniversary Address; July 1897, pp. 19–50: Paper by Isabella Bird Bishop on "A Journey in Western Sze-chuan" read at the RGS on May 10, 1897.

BETH URQUHART'S COLLECTION

Correspondence from Mary Kingsley

Mary Kingsley to:

Joseph Chamberlain	April 1898–September 1899
Christy	June 1897–October 1899
Edward Clodd	January–August 1898
Lord Cromer	September 1899
Thiselton Dyer	March 1896
Dr. Frazer	January–November 1899
Mrs Frazer	December 1899
Professor Haddon	May–July 1896
Mrs Haddon	May 1897
Hartland	December 1896–October 1899
Alice Stopford Green	February 1897–April 1900
Dr Günther	December 1894–October 1899
Stephen Gwynn	August 1898–February 1900
Mrs Gwynn	November 1898–June 1899
Ling Roth	November 1897–February 1900

Mrs Ling Roth	November 1897–February 1900
Sir Alfred Lyall	July 1897
E. D. Morel	February 1899–March 1900
John Holt	November 1897–March 1900
Major Nathan	February 1899–March 1900
St. Loe Strachey	February 1899–March 1900
Sir Edward Tylor	October 1896–October 1899
Mrs Tylor	October–December 1896

One letter from Mary Kingsley to Mrs Cowell (February 7, 1891) and Mrs Brownlow (1896); two letters to Miss Bowdler-Sharpe (January 31, 1897 and February 11, 1897).

Correspondence from Mary Kingsley to John Scott Keltie, George Macmillan, and Violet Paget Roy, as listed above.

Articles about Mary Kingsley

Athenaeum	January 27, 1900
	June 9, 1900
	June 16, 1900
	June 23, 1900
Mainly about People	June 16, 1900
Outlook	June 9, 1900

Beth Urquhart's collection also includes other articles about Mary Kingsley and notes from diverse secondary sources that I have not referred to in my account of Mary Kingsley.

Secondary Source Material

Adams, P. *Travel Literature and the Evolution of the Novel*. Lexington: University Press of Kentucky, 1983.

Ahmed, L. "Western Ethnocentrism and Perceptions of the Harem." *Feminist Studies* 8, 3 (1982): 521–534.

Alcoff, L. "Cultural Feminism versus Post-Structuralism: The Identity Crisis in Feminist Theory." *Signs* 13, 3 (1988): 405–437.

Alexander, C. *One Dry Season: In the Footsteps of Mary Kingsley*. New York: Vintage, 1991.

Allen, A. *Travelling Ladies*. London: Jupiter, 1980.

Ardis, A. L. *New Women, New Novels: Feminism and Early Modernism*. New Brunswick, NJ: Rutgers University Press, 1990.

Armstrong, N., and Tennenhouse, L., eds. *The Ideology of Conduct: Essays in Literature and the History of Sexuality*. New York: Methuen, 1987.

Asad, T. "Anthropology and the Colonial Encounter," in G. Huizer and B. Mannheim eds. *The Politics of Anthropology: From Colonialism and Sexism toward a View from Below*. The Hague: Mouton, 1979.

Attridge, D., Bennington, G., and Young, R., eds. *Post-structuralism and the Question of History*. Cambridge, England: Cambridge University Press, 1987.

Balibar, E., and Macherey, P. "On Literature as an Ideological Form," in R. Young, ed. *Untying the Text: A Post-structuralist Reader*. Boston: Routledge and Kegan Paul, 1981.

Barr, P. *A Curious Life for a Lady: The Story of Isabella Bird, Traveller Extraordinary*. London: Penguin, 1986.

Barthes, R. *The Pleasure of the Text*, trans. R. Miller. New York: Hill and Wang, 1975.

Batten, C. *Pleasurable Instruction: Form and Convention in Eighteenth Century Travel Literature*. Berkeley: University of California Press, 1978.

Bhabha, H. K. "The Other Question. . . ." *Screen* 24, 6 (1983): 18–36.

Bhabha, H. K. "Representation and the Colonial Text: A Critical Exploration of Some Forms of Mimeticism," in F. Gloversmith, ed. *The Theory of Reading*. Brighton, England: Harvester Press, 1984.

Bhabha, H. K. "Signs Taken for Wonders: Questions of Ambivalence and Authority under a Tree Outside Delhi, May 1817." *Critical Inquiry* 12 (1985): 144–165.

Bhabha, H. K. "Articulating the Archaic: Notes on Colonial Nonsense," in P. Collier and H. Geyer-Ryan, eds. *Literary Theory Today*. Ithaca, NY: Cornell University Press, 1990.

Bhabha, H. K. "The World and the Home." *Social Text* 31/32 (1992): 141–153.

Birkett, D. "An Independent Woman in West Africa: The Case of Mary Kingsley." Ph.D. thesis, University of London, 1987.

Birkett, D. *Spinsters Abroad: Victorian Lady Explorers*. Oxford, England: Basil Blackwell, 1989.

Birkett, D. *Mary Kingsley—Imperial Adventuress*. London: Macmillan, 1992.

Birkett, D., and Wheelwright, J. "'How Could She?' Unpalatable Facts and Feminists' Heroines." *Gender and History* 2, 1 (1990): 49–57.

Blake, S. L. "A Woman's Trek: What Difference Does Gender Make?" *Women's Studies International Forum* 13, 4 (1990): 347-355.

Blake, S. L. "Travel and Literature: The Liberian Narratives of Esther Warner and Graham Greene." *Research in African Literatures* 22, 2 (1991): 191-203.

Blunt, A. "Mapping Authorship and Authority: Reading Mary Kingsley's Landscape Descriptions," in A. Blunt, and G. Rose, ed. *Sexual/Textual Colonizations: Women's Colonial and Post-colonial Geographies*. New York: Guilford Press, forthcoming.

Blunt A., and Rose, G. "Introduction: Women's Colonial and Post-colonial Geographies," in A. Blunt and G. Rose, eds. *Sexual/Textual Colonizations: Women's Colonial and Post-colonial Geographies*. New York: Guilford Press, forthcoming.

Blythe, M. "'What's in a Name?' Film Culture and the Self/Other Question." *Quarterly Review of Film and Video* 13 (1991): 205-215.

Bondi, L., and Domosh, M. "Other Figures in Other Places: On Feminism, Postmodernism and Geography." *Environment and Planning D: Society and Space* 10 (1992): 199-213.

Brantlinger, P. "Victorians and Africans: The Genealogy of the Myth of the Dark Continent." *Critical Inquiry* 12 (1985): 166-203.

Brantlinger, P. *Rule of Darkness: British Literature and Imperialism, 1830-1914*. Ithaca, NY: Cornell University Press, 1988.

Burkin, E., Pratt, M. B., and Smith, B., eds. *Yours in Struggle*. Ithaca, NY: Firebrand Books, 1984.

Burton, A. M. "The White Woman's Burden: British Feminists and the Indian Woman, 1865-1915." *Women's Studies International Forum* 13, 4 (1990): 295-308. Reprinted in N. Chaudhuri, and M. Strobel, eds. *Western Women and Imperialism: Complicity and Resistance*. Bloomington: Indiana University Press, 1992.

Busia, A.P.A. "Miscegenation as Metonymy: Sexuality and Power in the Colonial Novel." *Ethnic and Racial Studies* 9 (1986): 360-372.

Callaway, H., and Helly, D. O. "Crusader for Empire: Flora Shaw/Lady Lugard," in N. Chaudhuri and M. Strobel, eds. *Western Women and Imperialism: Complicity and Resistance*. Bloomington: Indiana University Press, 1992.

Campbell, M. *The Witness and the Other World: Exotic European Travel Writing, 400-1600*. Ithaca, NY: Cornell University Press, 1988.

Campbell, O. *Mary Kingsley: A Victorian in the Jungle*. London: Methuen, 1957.

Careless, V. "The Ethnological Society of London, 1843-1871." M.A. thesis, University of British Columbia, 1974.

Carter, P. *The Road to Botany Bay: An Essay in Spatial History*. London: Faber and Faber, 1987.

Carter, P. *Living in a New Country: History, Travelling and Language*. London: Faber and Faber, 1992.

Chaudhuri, N., and Strobel, M. "Western Women and Imperialism: Introduction." *Women's Studies International Forum* 13, 4 (1990): 289–293.

Chaudhuri, N., and Strobel, M., eds. *Western Women and Imperialism: Complicity and Resistance*. Bloomington: Indiana University Press, 1992.

Clifford, J. *The Predicament of Culture: Twentieth Century Ethnography, Literature and Art*. Cambridge, MA: Harvard University Press, 1988.

Clifford, J. "Travelling Cultures," in L. Grossberg, C. Nelson, and P. Triechler, eds. *Cultural Studies*. London: Routledge, 1992.

Clifford, J., and Marcus, G. E., eds. *Writing Culture: The Poetics and Politics of Ethnography*. Berkeley: University of California Press, 1986.

Clodd, E. *Memories*. London: Chapman and Hall, 1916.

Collier, P., and Geyer-Ryan, H., eds. *Literary Theory Today*. Ithaca, NY: Cornell University Press, 1990.

Culler, J. *Framing the Sign: Criticism and Its Institutions*. Norman: University of Oklahoma Press, 1988.

Davenport Adams, W. H. *Celebrated Women Travellers of the Nineteenth Century*. London: W. Swan Sonnenschein, 1883.

Davenport Adams, W. H. *Celebrated Englishwomen of the Victorian Era*. 2 vols. London: F. V. White, 1884.

Davidson, L. C. *Hints to Lady Travellers at Home and Abroad*. London: Iliffe, 1889.

Davis, L. *Resisting Novels: Ideology and Fiction*. New York: Methuen, 1987.

de Certeau, M. *The Practice of Everyday Life*, trans. S. Randall. Berkeley: University of California Press, 1984.

De Groot, J. "'Sex' and 'Race': The Construction of Language and Image in the Nineteenth Century," in S. Mendus, and J. Rendall, eds. *Sexuality and Subordination: Interdisciplinary Studies of Gender in the Nineteenth Century*. London: Routledge, 1989.

Doane, M. A. *The Desire to Desire*. Bloomington: Indiana University Press, 1987.

Dodd, P., ed. *The Art of Travel: Essays on Travel Writing*. London: Frank Cass, 1982.

Domosh, M. "Toward a Feminist Historiography of Geography." *Transactions of the Institute of British Geographers* N.S. 16 (1991a): 95–104.

Domosh, M. "Beyond the Frontiers of Geographical Knowledge." *Trans-*

actions of the Institute of British Geographers N.S. 16 (1991b): 488–490.

Driver, F. "Geography's Empire: Histories of Geographical Knowledge." *Environment and Planning D: Society and Space* 10 (1992): 23–40.

Driver, F., and Rose, G., eds. *Nature and Science: Essays in the History of Geographical Knowledge*. London: Historical Geography Research Group of the Institute of British Geographers, 1992.

Duncan, J. *The City as Text—The Politics of Landscape Interpretation in the Kandyan Kingdom*. Cambridge, England: Cambridge University Press, 1990.

Fabian, J. "Presence and Representation: The Other and Anthropological Writing." *Critical Inquiry* 16, 4 (1990): 753–772.

Flint, J. E. "Mary Kingsley: A Reassessment." *Journal of African History* 6, 1 (1963): 95–104.

Foucault, M. "What Is an Author?" in J. V. Harari, ed. *Textual Strategies: Perspectives in Poststructuralist Criticism*. Ithaca, NY: Cornell University Press, 1979.

Foucault, M. *The History of Sexuality*, vol. 1. trans. R. Hurley. New York: Vintage Books, 1990.

Frank, K. *A Voyager Out: The Life of Mary Kingsley*. Boston: Houghton Mifflin, 1986a.

Frank, K. "Voyages Out: Nineteenth Century Women Travelers in Africa," in J. Sharistanian, ed. *Gender, Ideology and Action: Historical Perspectives on Women's Public Lives*. New York: Greenwood Press, 1986b.

Freshfield, D. W., and Wharton, W. J. L., eds. *Hints to Travellers Scientific and General*. 7th ed. London: Royal Geographical Society, 1893.

Fussell, P. *Abroad: British Literary Traveling Between the Wars*. Oxford, England: Oxford University Press, 1980.

Galton, F. *The Art of Travel; or, Shifts and Contrivances Available in Wild Countries*. 7th ed. London: John Murray, 1883.

Gilman, S. L. "Black Bodies, White Bodies: Toward an Iconography of Female Sexuality in Late Nineteenth Century Art, Medicine, and Literature." *Critical Inquiry* 12 (1985): 204–242.

Gloversmith, F., ed. *The Theory of Reading*. Brighton, England: Harvester Press, 1984.

Grossberg, L., Nelson, C., and Treichler, P., eds. *Cultural Studies*. London: Routledge, 1992.

Gwynn, S. *The Life of Mary Kingsley*. Harmondsworth: Penguin, 1940.

Haggis, J. "Gendering Colonialism or Colonising Gender? Recent Women's Studies Approaches to White Women and the History of British Colonialism." *Women's Studies International Forum* 13 (1990): 105–115.

Hall, J., and Abbas, A., eds. *Literature and Anthropology*. Hong Kong: Hong Kong University Press, 1986.

Hamalian, L., ed. *Ladies on the Loose: Women Travellers of the Eighteenth and Nineteenth Centuries*. New York: Dodd and Mead, 1981.

Harari, J. V., ed. *Textual Strategies: Perspectives in Poststructuralist Criticism*. Ithaca, NY: Cornell University Press, 1979.

Hassam, A. "'As I Write': Narrative Occasions and the Quest for Self-Presence in the Travel Diary." *Ariel* 21, 4 (October 1990): 33–47.

Hayford, M. C. *Mary H. Kingsley: From an African Standpoint*. London: Bear and Taylor, 1901.

Hekman, S. "Reconstituting the Subject: Feminism, Modernism, and Postmodernism." *Hypatia* 6, 2 (1991): 44–63.

Hibbert, C. *Africa Explored: Europeans in the Dark Continent, 1769-1889*. Harmondsworth: Penguin, 1982.

H.M.L.S. *A Few Words of Advice on Travelling and Its Requirements Addressed to Ladies*, 4th ed. London: Thomas Cook, 1878.

Holmlund, C. A. "Displacing Limits of Difference: Gender, Race, and Colonialism in Edward Said and Homi Bhabha's Theoretical Models and Marguerite Duras's Experimental Films." *Quarterly Review of Film and Video* 13 (1991): 1–22.

hooks, b. *Yearning: Race, Gender and Cultural Politics*. Boston: South End Press, 1990.

hooks, b. "Representing Whiteness in the Black Imagination," in L. Grossberg, C. Nelson, and P. Treichler, eds. *Cultural Studies*. London: Routledge, 1992.

Howard, J. "Feminism and the Question of History: Resituating the Debate." *Women's Studies* 19 (1991): 149–157.

Howell, M. C. "A New Feminist Historian Looks at the New Historicism: What's so Historical about It?" *Women's Studies* 19 (1991): 139–147.

Huggan, G. "Maps and Mapping Strategies in Contemporary Canadian and Australian Fiction." Ph.D. thesis, University of British Columbia, 1989.

Huizer, G., and Mannheim, B., eds. *The Politics of Anthropology: From Colonialism and Sexism Toward a View from Below*. The Hague: Mouton, 1979.

Hutchinson, S. *Cervantine Journeys*. Madison: University of Wisconsin Press, 1992.

JanMohamed, A. R. "The Economy of Manichean Allegory: The Function of Racial Difference in Colonialist Literature." *Critical Inquiry* 12 (1985): 59–87.

Kabbani, R. *Europe's Myths of Orient: Devise and Rule*. London: Macmillan, 1986.

Kaplan, C. "Deterritorializations: The Rewriting of Home and Exile in Western Feminist Discourse." *Cultural Critique* 6 (1987): 187–198.

Kingsley, G.H. *Notes on Sport and Travel*. London: Macmillan, 1900.

Kroller, E. M. "First Impressions: Rhetorical Strategies in Travel Writing by Victorian Women." *Ariel* 21, 4 (1990): 87–99.

Kyle, N. "Cara David and the 'Truths' of Her 'Unscientific' Travellers' Tales in Australia and the South Pacific." *Women's Studies International Forum* 16, 2 (1993): 105–118.

Laurenson, D., ed. *The Sociology of Literature*. Sociological Review Monograph 26. Keele, England: University of Keele, 1978.

Livingstone, D. *The Geographical Tradition: Episodes in the History of a Contested Enterprise*. Oxford, England: Basil Blackwell, 1993.

Lloyd, G. *The Man of Reason ; 'Male' and 'Female' in Western Philosophy*. London: Methuen, 1984.

Loomba, A. "Overworlding the 'Third World.'" *Oxford Literary Review* 13 (1991): 164–191.

Lowe, L. *Critical Terrains: French and British Orientalisms*. Ithaca, NY: Cornell University Press, 1991.

MacCannell, D. *The Tourist*. New York: Schocken, 1976.

McEwan, C. "Encounters with West African Women: Authority and Constraints in the Texts of Victorian Women Travel Writers," in A. Blunt and G. Rose, eds. *Sexual/Textual Colonizations: Women's Colonial and Post-colonial Geographies*. New York: Guilford, forthcoming.

MacKenzie, J. "Geography and Imperialism: British Provincial Geographical Societies," in F. Driver and G. Rose, eds. *Nature and Science: Essays in the History of Geographical Knowledge*.

MacLaren, I. S. "Introduction." *Ariel* 21, 4 (1990): 5–7.

McNay, L. *Foucault and Feminism: Power, Gender and the Self*. Cambridge, England: Polity Press, 1992.

Mabro, J., ed. *Half-veiled Truths: Western Travellers' Perceptions of Middle Eastern Women*. London: I. B. Tauris, 1991.

Mani, L., and Frankenberg, R. "The Challenge of Orientalism." *Economy and Society* 14, 2 (1985): 174–192.

Marangoly George, R. M. "Traveling Light: Of Immigration, Invisible Suitcases, and Gunny Sacks." *Differences* 4, 2 (1992): 72–99.

Marcus, J. "Predicated on Gender." *Social Analysis* 29 (1990): 136–144.

Martin, B., and Mohanty, C. T. "Feminist Politics: What's Home Got to Do with It?" in T. de Lauretis, ed. *Feminist Studies/Critical Studies*. Bloomington: Indiana University Press, 1986.

Martin, B. *Woman and Modernity: The (Life)Styles of Lou Andreas-Salomé*. Ithaca, NY: Cornell University Press, 1991.

Melman, B. *Women's Orients: English Women and the Middle East, 1718–1918: Sexuality, Religion and Work*. London: Macmillan, 1992.

Middleton, D. *Victorian Lady Travellers*. London: Routledge and Kegan Paul, 1965.

Middleton, D. "Some Victorian Lady Travellers," *Geographical Journal* 139 (1973): 65–75.

Middleton, D. "Francis Galton: Victorian Genius." *Geographical Journal* 141, 2 (1975): 266–269.

Mills, S. "Discourses of Difference." *Cultural Studies* 4, 2 (1990): 128–140.

Mills, S. *Discourses of Difference: An Analysis of Women's Travel Writing and Colonialism*. London: Routledge, 1991.

Minh-ha, T. T. *Woman, Native, Other: Writing Postcoloniality and Feminism*. Bloomington: Indiana University Press, 1989.

Mitchell, T. *Colonizing Egypt*. Cambridge, England: Cambridge University Press, 1988.

Moers, E. *Literary Women*. London: Women's Press, 1978.

Mohanty, C. T. "Under Western Eyes: Feminist Scholarship and Colonial Discourses." *Boundary* 2, 3 (1984): 333–358.

Morgan, C. L. *The House of MacMillan 1843–1943*. London: Macmillan, 1943.

Morgan, S. "An Introduction to Victorian Women's Travel Writings about Southeast Asia." *Genre* 20 (1987): 189–208.

Morris, M. "At Henry Parkes Motel." *Cultural Studies* 2, 1 (1988): 1–16 and 29–47.

Mulvey, L. *Visual and Other Pleasures*. Basingstoke, England: Macmillan, 1989.

Newton, J. "History as Usual? Feminism and the 'New Historicism.'" *Cultural Critique* 9 (1988): 87–121.

Nworah, K. D. "The Liverpool 'Sect' and British West African Policy 1895–1915." *African Affairs* 70, 281 (1971): 349–365.

Pakenham, T. *The Scramble for Africa, 1876–1912*. London: Weidenfeld and Nicolson, 1991.

Parry, B. "Problems in Current Theories of Colonial Discourse." *Oxford Literary Review* 9 (1987): 27–58.

Pearce, R. D. *Mary Kingsley: Light at the Heart of Darkness*. Oxford, England: Kensal, 1990.

Pile, S., and Rose, G. "All or Nothing? Politics and Critique in the Modernism-Postmodernism Debate." *Environment and Planning D: Society and Space* 10 (1992): 123–136.

Pollock, G. *Vision and Difference: Femininity, Feminism and Histories of Art*. London: Routledge, 1988.

Poovey, M. *The Proper Lady and the Woman Writer: Ideology as Style in the Works of Mary Wollstonecraft, Mary Shelley, and Jane Austen.* Chicago: University of Chicago Press, 1984.

Poovey, M. *Uneven Developments: The Ideological Work of Gender in Mid-Victorian England.* Chicago: University of Chicago Press, 1988.

Pratt, G. "Commentary: Spatial Metaphors and Speaking Positions." *Environment and Planning D: Society and Space* 10 (1992): 241–244.

Pratt, M. B. "Identity: Skin Blood Heart," in E. Burkin, M. B. Pratt, and B. Smith, eds. *Yours in Struggle.* Ithaca, NY: Firebrand Books, 1984.

Pratt, M. L. "Scratches on the Face of the Country; or, What Mr. Barrow Saw in the Land of the Bushmen." *Critical Inquiry* 12 (1985): 119–143.

Pratt, M. L. "Fieldwork in Common Places," in J. Clifford and G. E. Marcus, eds. *Writing Culture: The Poetics and Politics of Ethnography.* Berkeley: University of California Press, 1986.

Pratt, M. L. "'Killed by Science': Travel Narrative and Ethnographic Writing," in J. Hall and A. Abbas, eds. *Literature and Anthropology.* Hong Kong: Hong Kong University Press, 1986b.

Pratt, M. L. *Imperial Eyes: Travel Writing and Transculturation.* London: Routledge, 1992.

Radhakrishnan, R. "Feminist Historiography and Post-structuralist Thought," in E. Meese and A. Parker, eds. *The Difference Within: Feminism and Critical Theory.* Amsterdam: John Benjamins, 1989.

Richards, T. *The Commodity Culture of Victorian England: Advertising and Spectacle, 1851–1914.* Stanford: Stanford University Press, 1990.

Riley, D. *'Am I That Name?' Feminism and the Category of 'Women' in History.* London: Macmillan, 1988.

Roberts, H. "Propaganda and Ideology in Women's Fiction," in D. Laurenson, ed. *The Sociology of Literature,* Sociological Review Monograph 26. Keele, England: University of Keele, 1978.

Robinson, J. *Wayward Women: A Guide to Women Travellers.* Oxford, England: Oxford University Press, 1990.

Robinson, R., and Gallagher, J. *Africa and the Victorians.* New York: St. Martin's Press, 1961.

Rose, G. "Geography as a Science of Observation: The Landscape, the Gaze and Masculinity," in F. Driver and G. Rose, eds. *Essays in the History of Geographical Knowledge.* London: Historical Geography Research Group of the Institute of British Geographers, 1992.

Rose, G. *Feminism and Geography: The Limits of Geographical Knowledge.* Cambridge, England: Polity Press, 1993.

Rose, G., and Ogborn, M. "Feminism and Historical Geography." *Journal of Historical Geography* 14, 4 (1988): 405–409.

Rose, J. *Sexuality in the Field of Vision*. London: Verso, 1986.

Russell, M. *The Blessings of a Good Thick Skirt: Women Travellers and Their World*. London: Collins, 1988.

Said, E. W. *Orientalism*. New York: Vintage Books, 1979.

Said, E. W. *The World, the Text, and the Critic*. Cambridge, MA: Harvard University Press, 1983.

Said, E. W. "Orientalism Reconsidered." *Cultural Critique* 1 (1985): 89–107.

Said, E. W. *Culture and Imperialism*. New York: Alfred A. Knopf, 1993.

Schaffer, K. *Women and the Bush: Forces of Desire in the Australian Cultural Tradition*. Cambridge, England: Cambridge University Press, 1990.

Scott, J. W. "Deconstructing Equality-Versus-Difference: or, The Uses of Poststructuralist Theory for Feminism." *Feminist Studies* 14, 1 (1988a): 33–50.

Scott, J. W. *Gender and the Politics of History*. New York: Columbia University Press, 1988b.

Sharistanian, J., ed. *Gender, Ideology and Action: Historical Perspectives on Women's Public Lives*. New York: Greenwood Press, 1986.

Shattock, J. "Travel Writing Victorian and Modern: A Review of Recent Research," in P. Dodd, ed. *The Art of Travel: Essays on Travel Writing*. London: Frank Cass, 1982.

Sheridan, S. "'Wives and Mothers like Ourselves, Poor Remnants of a Dying Race': Aborigines in Colonial Women's Writing." *Kunapipi* 10 (1988): 76–91.

Shohat, E. "Gender and Culture of Empire: Toward a Feminist Ethnography of the Cinema." *Quarterly Review of Film and Video* 13 (1991): 45–84.

Showalter, E. *A Literature of Their Own: Women Novelists from Brontë to Lessing*. Princeton, NJ: Princeton University Press, 1977.

Spivak, G. C. "Three Women's Texts and a Critique of Imperialism." *Critical Inquiry* 12 (1985): 243–261.

Spivak, G. C. *The Post-colonial Critic: Interviews, Strategies, Dialogues*, ed. S. Harasym. London: Routledge, 1990.

Stevenson, C. *Victorian Women Travel Writers in Africa*. Boston: Twayne, 1982.

Stocking, G. W. *Victorian Anthropology*. New York: Free Press, 1987.

Stoddart, D. R. *On Geography and Its History*. Oxford, England: Basil Blackwell, 1986.

Stoddart, D. R. "Do We Need a Feminist Historiography of Geography—and if We Do, What Should It Be?" *Transactions of the Institute of British Geographers* N.S. 16 (1991): 484–487.

Stratton, J. *Writing Sites: A Genealogy of the Postmodern World.* London: Harvester Wheatsheaf, 1990.

Strobel, M. *European Women and the Second British Empire.* Bloomington: Indiana University Press, 1991.

Tinling, M. *Women into the Unknown: A Sourcebook of Women Explorers and Travellers.* New York: Greenwood Press, 1989.

Tompkins, J. P., ed. *Reader-Response Criticism: From Formalism to Poststructuralism.* Baltimore: Johns Hopkins University Press, 1980.

Turner, L. "Feminism, Femininity and Ethnographic Authority." *Women: A Cultural Review* 2, 3 (1991): 238-254.

Tylor, E. B. *Anthropology: An Introduction to the Study of Man and Civilization.* London: Macmillan, 1892.

Urry, J. *The Tourist Gaze: Leisure and Travel in Contemporary Societies.* London: Sage, 1990.

Valverde, M. "Poststructuralist Gender Historians: Are We Those Names?" *Labour/Le Travail* 25 (1990): 227-236.

Van den Abbeele, G. "Sightseers: The Tourist as Theorist." *Diacritics* 10 (1980): 2-14.

Van den Abbeele, G. *Travel as Metaphor: From Montaigne to Rousseau.* Minneapolis: University of Minnesota Press, 1992.

Van Wyk Smith, M. "'Arbitrary Rule' and the Eighteenth Century Discourse of Guinea." *Ariel* 21, 4 (1990): 119-137.

Walker, C. "Feminist Literary Criticism and the Author." *Critical Inquiry* 16, 3 (1990): 551-571.

Walker, C. "Persona Criticism and the Death of the Author," in W. H. Epstein, ed. *Contesting the Subject: Essays in the Postmodern Theory and Practice of Biography and Biographical Criticism.* West Lafayette, IN: Purdue University Press, 1991.

Ware, V. *Beyond the Pale: White Women, Racism and History.* London: Verso, 1992.

Weedon, C. *Feminist Practice and Poststructuralist Theory.* Oxford, England: Basil Blackwell, 1987.

West, R. *Brazza of the Congo—European Exploration and Exploitation in French Equatorial Africa.* London: Jonathan Cape, 1972.

Wolff, J. "On the Road Again: Metaphors of Travel in Cultural Criticism." *Cultural Studies* 7 (1993): 224-239.

Young, R., ed. *Untying the Text: A Post-structuralist Reader.* Boston: Routledge and Kegan Paul, 1981.

Young, R. *White Mythologies: Writing History and the West.* London: Routledge, 1990.

Women Fellows of the Royal Geographical Society, 1892–1893

Name	Description	Date Elected
Mrs. Isabella Bird Bishop	Widow, traveler, author	November 28, 1892
Mrs. Zelie Isabelle Colville	Wife of . . .	November 28, 1892
Miss Maria Vere Cust	Late Honorary Assistant Secretary to the International Oriental Congress 1892	November 28, 1892
Mrs. Cottereu Dormer	N.A.	November 28, 1892
Miss S. Agnes Darbishire	N.A.	November 28, 1892
Mrs. Lilly Grove	Lecturer and teacher of modern languages	N.A.
Miss E. Grey	Spinster	March 29, 1893
Mrs. Edward Patten Jackson	Widow, traveler, mountaineer	November 28, 1892
Mrs. Beatrice Hope Johnstone	Wife of . . .	November 28, 1892
Miss Julia Lindley	N.A.	February 27, 1893
Miss Kate Marsden	Spinster	November 28, 1892
Mrs. Edward Maberley	Widow	November 28, 1892
Mrs. Julia Machenna	Widow	January 16, 1893

Name	Description	Date Elected
Mrs. Juliet Mylne	Widow	November 28, 1892
Mrs. Elizabeth Mortimer	Wife of . . .	February 13, 1893
Mrs. Nicholas O'Connor	N.A.	November 28, 1892
Mrs. Mary Louisa O'Donoghue	Wife of . . .	March 13, 1893
Mrs. Emmeline Porcher	Widow	November 28, 1892
Miss Christina Rivington	Of Lady Margaret Hall College, Oxford; traveler in Egypt and Asia	November 28, 1892
Mrs. French Sheldon	Traveler in Africa	November 28, 1892
Miss Florence M. Small	Governess	N.A.
Lady Fox Young	N.A.	November 28, 1892

NOTE

1. N.A., not available. "Wife of [husband's name]" was the extent of some women's descriptions. Source: Certificates of Candidature for Election; from the "Ladies Box" of RGS Additional Papers 93–99. These certificates read, "We, the undersigned, recommend him as likely to become a useful and valuable Fellow." Eleven of the 22 women listed above changed "him" to "her."

Ollscoil na hÉireann, Gaillimh

3 1111 40078 9580